Sue Kim

16 Handmade Projects

Baby Boutique

Shoes, Hats, Bags, Toys & More

stashBOOKS.

an imprint of C&T Publishing

Text and Photography copyright © 2013 by Sue Kim

Photography and Artwork copyright © 2013 by C&T Publishing, Inc.

Publisher: Amy Marson

Creative Director: Gailen Runge

Art Director: Kristy Zacharias

Editors: Liz Aneloski and Lee Jonsson

Technical Editors: Ann Haley
and Susan Hendrickson

Cover/Book Designer: April Mostek

Production Coordinator: Rue Flaherty

Production Editors: Joanna Burgarino
and Katie Van Amburg

Illustrator: Kirstie Pettersen

Photo Assistant: Mary Peyton Peppo

Flat Subject Photography by Diane Pedersen of C&T Publishing, Inc., unless otherwise noted; Style Photography by Christina Straw, unless otherwise noted; How-to Photography by Sue Kim, unless otherwise noted

Published by Stash Books, an imprint of C&T Publishing, Inc., P.O. Box 1456, Lafayette, CA 94549

Library of Congress Cataloging-in-Publication Data

Kim, Sue, 1969-

Baby boutique : 16 handmade projects - shoes, hats, bags, toys & more / Sue Kim.

    pages cm

ISBN 978-1-60705-721-5 (soft cover)

1. Infants' clothing. 2. Infants' supplies. 3. Sewing. I. Title.

TT637.K55 2013

646.4'06--dc23

                    2013008183

Printed in China

10 9 8 7 6 5 4 3 2 1

Dedication

To all my customers and sewing friends who have encouraged me to write this new book, thank you for the gratitude you have shown for my patterns and for letting me know of your heartfelt desire to craft handmade items. To you I dedicate this book.

Acknowledgments

During the process of writing this book, I was encouraged by my dear husband, who provided me with wise counsel; and by my three lovely children, Chan, Caleb, and Veronica, who are a source of much of my energy. I am grateful for my close and talented friend June, who helped me make all the samples for the book; for Calvin, who was always a tremendous help; and for Patrick, Betty, and Glenda, too. Finally, to C&T's Liz and Ann, I am grateful for all the helpful ideas and suggestions you provided.

Contents

82

95

111

Introduction

One of the most dramatic changes in a woman's life is becoming a mother. To remember, congratulate, and acknowledge this event with a handmade gift for the mother and the baby—what else could be more beautiful?

The inspiration for this book came from emails by my customers, friends, and fellow sewists. I have often been asked the question, "What is the best handmade gift to take to a baby shower?" or, "Are any good gift projects suitable for beginners?"

One thing that really surprised me was how many more people wanted to make and give handmade presents for baby showers than I had thought. I received many letters, emails, and comments on my website. Each and every one of these notes was precious to me. I felt the sender's heartwarming love for the baby and the parents. Knowing that my designs were helping to bring happiness delighted me. So, I wanted to do more.

I often found myself imagining going to a baby shower. What would I make as a gift? What kind of card would I send? How would I wrap the gift? No doubt, these are questions you too would ask.

I was getting more and more inspired, thinking of the many thoughtful souls who wanted to make handmade gifts for the baby and expectant mother. Baby booties, receiving blankets, dolls and toys, bibs, and more came to mind—and finally, my answer: this book!

But I couldn't stop with the handmade gifts. For me, when preparing a gift for someone, an equally important aspect is considering how to wrap it. Ideally, the wrapping should complement the gift. I try to avoid store-bought, single-use gift wrap; homemade, reusable wrapping is ideal for homemade gifts! Because of this, I have included a drawstring pouch pattern, designed for wrapping and packaging small items. You could also use the diaper bags to wrap larger gifts.

I hope you enjoy these projects.

Basic Information

Sewing and Quilting Terms

BACKSTITCHING
Sewing back and forth to secure the beginnings and ends of the sewing line.

BASTING
Long, loose stitches to temporarily hold two or more layers together before sewing. The longer the stitch and the less tension between the stitches, the easier it is to remove the basting when necessary.

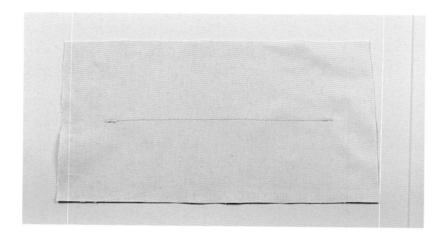

BIAS
A 45° angle to either the lengthwise or crosswise grain of a piece of fabric. It is the most elastic direction.

GRAIN
The lengthwise or crosswise direction of a piece of fabric.

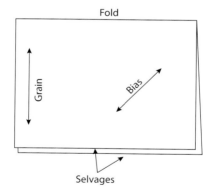

NOTCHING

Making small V-shaped cuts on the inner (concave seams) or outer (convex seams) curves to help them lie flat when turned to the right side. Always clip within the seam allowance; do not cut the stitches.

SEAM ALLOWANCE

The area between the raw edges of the layered fabric and the line of stitching. The width of the seam allowance may be different for each project.

SELVAGE

The finished edge of the fabric, usually printed with the designer's name, the producer's logo, and the colors used for the fabric represented in numbers.

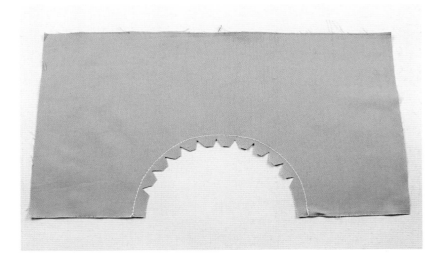

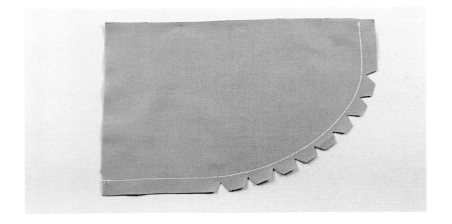

Basic Information

SLIP STITCH

The hidden stitching used when sewing an opening closed. This type of stitching is used to secure layers together almost invisibly by hiding the stitches between the layers. I prefer to use a double thread.

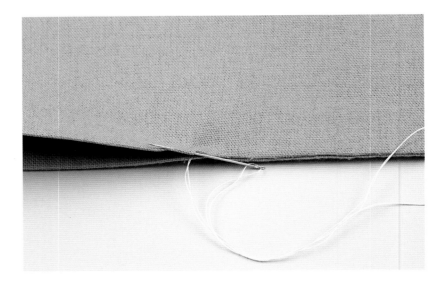

1. Use a thread color that matches your fabric, or use thread that is a shade darker to hide your stitches better. Thread a needle and knot the end of the thread. Insert the needle into the fold of the fabric and pull the thread taut to hide the knot between the layers of the fabric. Put the needle into the folded area from the inside to the outside and then insert the needle into the other side of the folded opening. Insert the needle along the fold; it shouldn't be inserted in a diagonal manner as the thread will become visible later on.

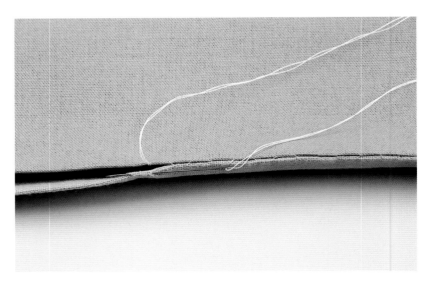

2. Pull the thread, then insert the needle into the fold of the opposite layer of fabric, and pull the thread taut. Repeat this process until the fabric is closed. Knot or secure with several stitches, and trim the thread.

STRAIGHT STITCH

This is the most simple and often-used form of stitching in sewing, also known as a running stitch.

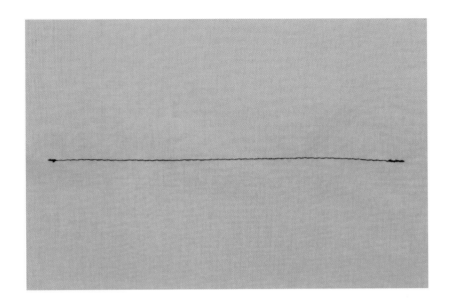

TOPSTITCHING

A line of machine stitching on the right side of the project used for reinforcement or decorative purposes. I like to use a fancy thread since it will show on the exposed side of the project.

Topstitching

Techniques

Applying Hook-and-Loop Tape

Hook-and-loop tape can be used instead of magnetic or sew-on snaps.

Cut the hook-and-loop tape to the desired length. Separate the hook-and-loop tape and place one piece onto the fabric. Sew around the edge of the hook-and-loop tape, backstitching at the beginning and end. Sew the corresponding hook-and-loop piece where indicated.

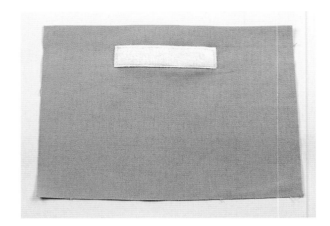

Attaching a Label

Applying a sewing label will result in a more personal project. Most commercial labels indicating the item is handmade are made of leather or cotton.

If the label is cotton, it can generally be attached in either of two ways. One way is to fold the edges under and baste or pin the label to the lining or exterior before sewing it onto your project. The other method is to sew the label to the lining or exterior after the project is completed. In both cases, be sure to use the same color thread as the label when sewing it together.

Don't have any labels? Consider using ribbons or your fabric selvages as a label. Cut off the selvages and keep them in a separate pile. Then you can use those saved selvages like a sewing label or ribbon, as I used the ribbon on the Bird Rattle (see Adding Ribbons, page 98).

Making Bias Strips

1. Using a ruler and cutting mat, cut strips as wide as desired at a 45° angle to the selvage.

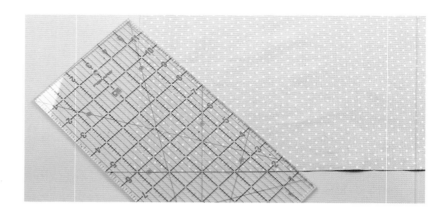

2. Place 2 strips with right sides together, meeting in an L shape as shown. Stitch at a 45° angle so they will make a straight strip when opened up. Add more strips until you have the desired length. Press the seams open. Trim the "rabbit ears" (the little triangles that stick out after pressing a diagonal seam).

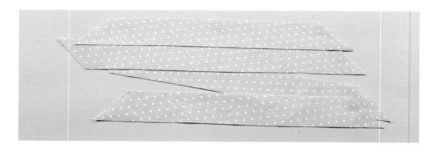

3. Press the strip in half lengthwise with wrong sides together. Open and fold the sides to meet at the crease. Fold in half again and press.

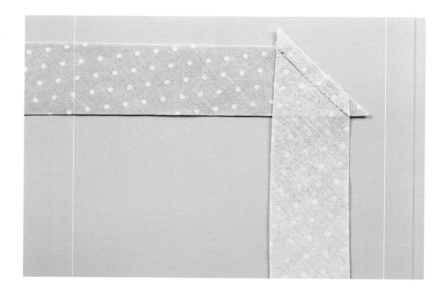

Drawing and Cutting the Shoe Pattern

Draw the patterns on the wrong side of a single layer of fabric. When tracing, remember that you need a right and a left shoe, so you will need to reverse the sole and some upper patterns. Use resealable bags to store the right and left pieces separately. This will help you avoid confusion when you assemble the pieces.

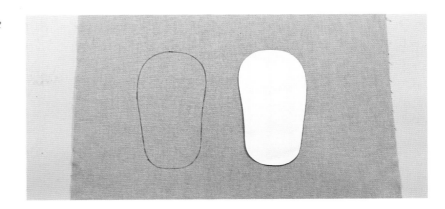

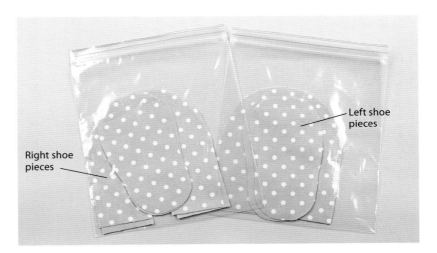

Right shoe pieces

Left shoe pieces

Tracing a Pattern

Place tracing paper on top of the pattern and hold the paper down with some sewing weights. Draw the pattern lines onto the tracing paper. During this time also write down the number of pieces to cut and transfer any markings such as darts. This will be convenient in the future because you won't need to refer to the instructions when making the item again. After tracing, copy it onto regular paper. You will use this regular paper as your pattern.

Making and Attaching Piping

Piping is a form of decorative trim or embellishment that can be purchased or made by hand.

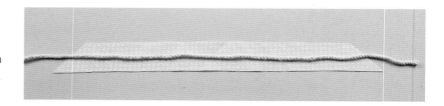

1. Cut and piece strips of fabric in the same way as described in Steps 1 and 2 in Making Bias Strips on page 14.

2. Place the cord on the wrong side in the center along the length of the bias strip. Fold the strip in half over the cord and align the raw edges. Pin in place.

3. Sew very close to the cord using a zipper foot or piping foot.

4. When applying piping to a corner, position the piping on the right side of the fabric, aligning the raw edges. Clip the seam allowance of the piping at the corner, as shown. For a round corner, notch the curved edges.

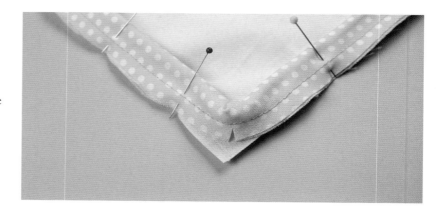

5. After adding the piping around the piece, to connect the 2 ends of the piping, cut 1 end and fold the piping fabric under ¼". Place the other end of the piping inside the folded edge. Pin in place and stitch.

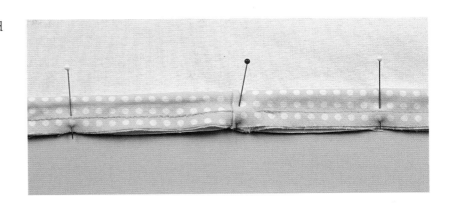

Making a Strap

1. Fold the strap piece in half lengthwise with wrong sides together and press.

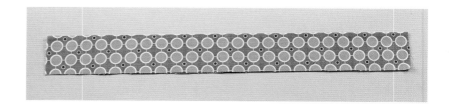

2. Open the strap and fold each side toward the center.

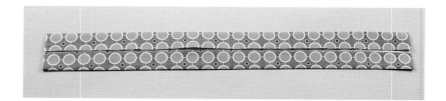

3. Fold along the center crease and press again.

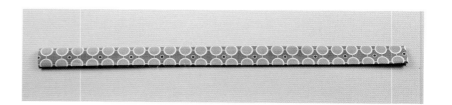

Making the Casing for Elastic

1. To create a casing for elastic, fold the top edge of the fabric piece under twice, following the project instructions.

2. Pin and sew along the fold line, backstitching at each end of the seam.

3. Attach a safety pin to one end of the elastic.

4. Insert the safety pin into an open end and work it through the casing.

5. Pull it through the opening on the other end, gathering the fabric.

6. Stitch to secure the ends of the elastic as directed in the project and cut off any excess.

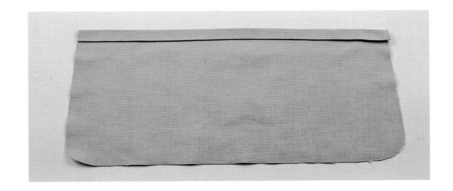

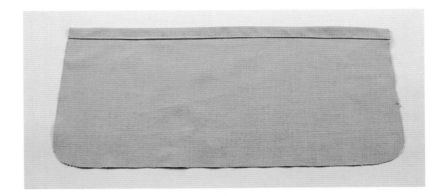

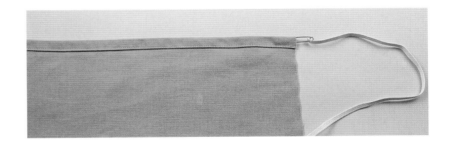

Using Iron-on Vinyl

When making projects like baby bibs or bags, it is convenient to use waterproof fabrics such as oilcloth or vinyl. If finding waterproof fabric is difficult, using iron-on vinyl is a good alternative. Fuse the vinyl to the right side of the exterior fabric, following the manufacturer's instructions.

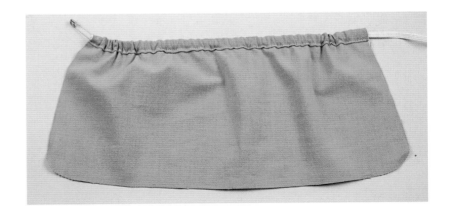

Tools

Acrylic Ruler

An acrylic ruler is a must-have tool when sewing. Acrylic rulers are used with a rotary cutter and cutting mat. Many different shapes and sizes are available. Choose a size that best fits your needs.

Chalk and Removable Marking Pens

Many types of tools make removable marks on fabric. Although what you choose is a personal preference, removable marking pens tend to be more precise and detailed than chalk, which tends to draw thicker lines and to smudge.

Cutting Mat

I recommend using a quilter's cutting mat designed for use with a rotary cutter. The cutting mat provides the user with various helpful lines and angles and therefore results in more precise cutting. The mat does not show any significant scratches or marks even after multiple slices and cuts with a rotary cutter.

Needles

The two basic types of needles are hand-sewing needles and sewing-machine needles. Be sure to purchase high-quality needles. Lower grade needles ruin fabric with their poor points.

Pincushion

A pincushion is helpful for placing pins and needles in one convenient area where they can be used and stored. Recently, magnetic pin dishes have become popular. However, if you are using a computerized sewing machine, you should keep magnets away from it, because the magnet may cause the machine to malfunction.

Pinking Shears

Pinking shears are designed to cut fabric and prevent the fabric from fraying. Pinking shears can make notching smoother and faster since there is no need to cut each of the notches individually. With a seam allowance wider than ¼", you may want to notch the fabric as well as pinking it to keep the seam from puckering.

Rotary Cutter

A rotary cutter is a tool that makes cutting fabrics very easy and smooth. For best results, the user needs to put an even amount of pressure on the blade when slicing. This takes some practice, but after a few tries, it will become second nature and you'll have another great sewing skill.

When cutting fabric with a rotary cutter, try to cut away from yourself rather than back and forth.

As a safety precaution, return the rotary cutter blade to its sheath after every use. Also be sure to store the rotary cutter and extra blades where children cannot reach them.

Scissors

Be sure to choose fabric shears when looking for scissors. Fabric shears are designed for the sole purpose of cutting fabrics. Try to find fabric shears with a handle that will be comfortable to use for long periods of time. This will make the cutting experience a better one! When the handles are uncomfortable, efficiency and precision fall off. Finally, to keep the fabric shears in good condition, they should be used only for cutting fabrics.

Seam Ripper

A seam ripper is a tool used to take out stitches easily. You will want to keep this tool handy.

Sewing Machine

All the patterns in the book can be made with any household sewing machine. If you would like to machine quilt, a sewing machine with a wide table will make the quilting go smoother.

It is nice to use a walking foot to keep the layers in place when you are quilting a quilt. When a walking foot is not available, it is possible to prevent the layers from shifting while quilting by holding the quilt firmly with a hand on each side of the area being stitched.

Fabric, Interfacing, and Thread

Fabric

For each project, choose fabrics that are appropriate for the intended use. Since babies have very sensitive skin, consider using organic fabrics. Fortunately, more manufacturers are producing organic fabrics in a variety of designs today. Below are the fabrics I recommend for the projects in this book.

FOR BABY SHOES:

+ Strong materials (such as home decor fabric) that are a blend of cotton and linen for the exterior fabric of the shoes.

+ Nonskid materials like suede for the soles, to provide traction and help prevent the toddler from slipping.

+ Quilting-weight cotton for the baby shoe lining.

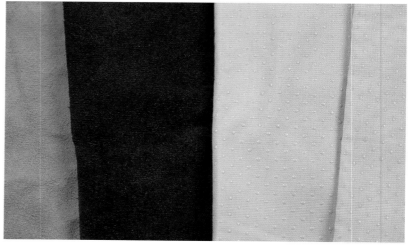

Suede, faux leather, and nonskid fabrics

FOR BABY BIBS:

+ Laminated, waterproof fabrics. These specialty fabrics can be purchased in fabric stores or via the Internet.

+ Quilting-weight or organic cotton for the lining, which will be in contact with the baby's skin.

Waterproof fabrics

FOR THE QUILT TOP AND BACKING:

+ Quilting-weight cotton. Consider looking for fat quarters and precuts (5″ × 5″, 10″ × 10″, and 2½″ × 44″ strips), which can reduce a lot of time when cutting pattern pieces for the projects. The precut packs usually include about 20–40 different fabrics.

+ Linen gives a natural and earthy feeling; however, using a linen or linen/cotton blend can result in a heavier look compared with quilting-weight cotton.

Organic blend fabrics

FOR BAGS, ESPECIALLY DIAPER BAGS:

✦ Durable fabrics such as home decor fabrics, since they are usually put to heavy use.

✦ Waterproof materials.

FOR THE TEDDY BEAR, DOLL, AND RATTLES:

✦ Plush, fleece, terry cloth, and microfiber. The dolls can also be made using felt or socks.

Terry cloth, plush, microfiber, and fleece

Interfacing

Use a soft fusible interfacing such as Shape-Flex by C&T Publishing.

Thread

When using a sewing machine, use an all-purpose thread. When sewing denim, use thread designed for heavyweight fabrics. Hand-quilting thread and embroidery floss are what I typically suggest for hand sewing.

Gift Ideas

When making baby gifts like the shoes or hats, it is important to think ahead of when and how long the baby will use the item. You can sew something for a newborn, but that allows the baby to wear it for only a limited time because they grow so quickly. If you want something the baby can wear longer, making something for size 6 to 12 months is a good idea. It is also a good idea to try to predict what season the baby will be wearing this item. By matching the season, you can choose appropriate fabric and materials. Regardless of the baby's age or the season, dolls, quilts, and bibs are great gifts.

CAUTION
Small children may choke on beads, buttons, snaps, and other small pieces if they come loose.

If one gift does not seem like it is enough to express your joy for the expectant family, try making a set of gifts. For example, you could make a pair of shoes and a hat, a hat and a bib, a bib and a rattle, a diaper bag and a pouch, a bag and a teddy bear, a teddy bear and a neck rest rattle, or a pair of baby shoes and a bib. Making multiple bibs is another suggestion. Anyone who has raised a child will know: No matter how many bibs you have, you can never have enough.

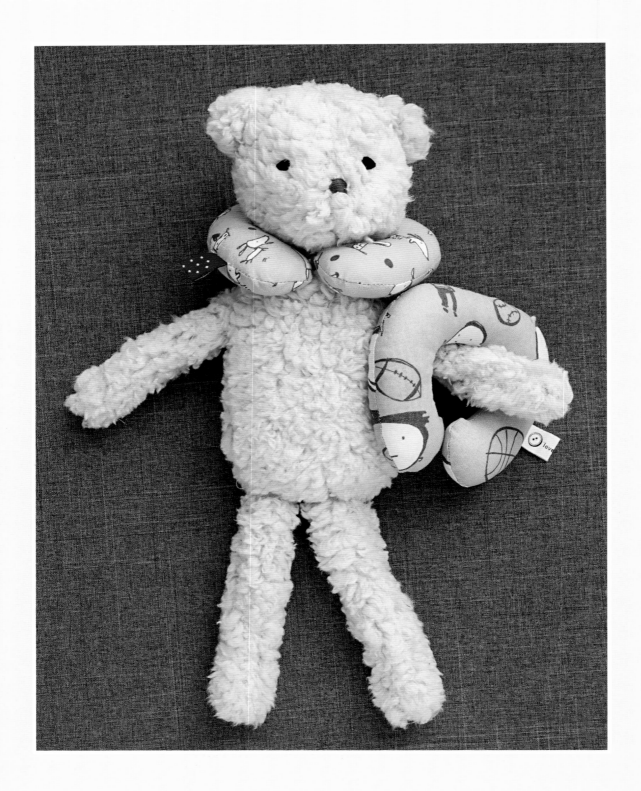

Baby Shoes

Christine Baby Mary Janes

FINISHED SIZE: U.S. baby shoe size 1–5 ◆ **SKILL LEVEL:** Beginner

The Christine Baby Mary Janes are made with higher ankles than the traditional Mary Jane shoes. Christine Baby Mary Janes can be made with a small amount of fabric and are great for crawling babies, indoor play, and stroller trips. Due to their size, they can even be made by hand, without a sewing machine. They are an affordable way to match your baby's footwear with her outfit, and they make an adorable gift for new moms or moms-to-be.

See pullout page P3 for the Christine Baby Mary Janes upper, sole, and petal patterns.

Materials

- ¼ yard 44″-wide home decor or quilting-weight cotton fabric (or 1 fat quarter) for exterior
- ¼ yard or 1 fat quarter quilting-weight cotton for lining
- ¼ yard of 44″-wide fusible interfacing, such as Shape-Flex by C&T Publishing
- 1½″ piece ½″-wide hook-and-loop tape
- 7″ × 12″ fabric for corsages (*optional*)
- Beads for corsages (*optional*)
- Invisible thread for attaching beads (*optional*)

Cutting

A ¼″ seam allowance is included on the patterns.

Trace the patterns on the wrong side of a single layer of fabric. For the pieces that require mirror-image pieces (1 and 1 reversed), use 2 layers of fabric placed right sides together.

See Drawing and Cutting the Shoe Pattern, page 15. Cut out the pattern pieces as follows.

EXTERIOR
Cut 2 upper pieces.

Cut 2 sole pieces (1 and 1 reversed).

Cut 2 strap pieces 2″ × 4½″ (size 1, 2, or 3) or 2¼″ × 5¼″ (size 4 or 5).

LINING
Cut 2 upper pieces.

Cut 4 sole pieces (2 and 2 reversed).

INTERFACING
Cut 2 upper pieces.

Cut 2 sole pieces (1 and 1 reversed).

CORSAGES
Cut 18 petals.

OTHER
Cut 2 pieces of hook-and-loop tape, ¾″ each.

Assembly

Use a ¼″ seam allowance unless otherwise directed.
Backstitch at the beginning and end of each seam.

Fusing the Interfacing

Fuse the interfacing on the wrong side of the corresponding lining pieces, following the manufacturer's instructions.

Sewing the Upper

1. Fold an exterior upper piece in half lengthwise with right sides together. Pin and sew the heel (FIGURE 1). Press the seam open. Sew the remaining exterior and lining upper pieces in the same manner.

2. Flip the exterior upper right side out and place the lining upper piece on top with right sides together. Pin the 2 pieces together around the inner edge. Sew along the inner edge (FIGURE 2).

3. Notch the top of the heel seam and around the inner seam (FIGURE 3).

4. Turn the assembled upper right side out and press around the top (FIGURE 4).

5. Repeat Steps 1–4 to construct the upper for the other shoe.

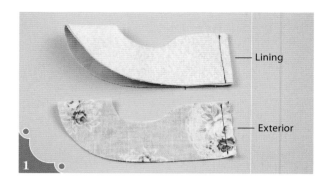

Lining

Exterior

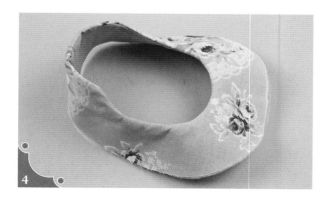

Sewing the Upper and Sole

1. Place the assembled upper and the exterior sole pieces together with the exterior right sides facing, matching their center points. Pin the toe and heel (FIGURE 5).

2. Pin around one side of the sole. Then, pin around the rest of the sole (FIGURE 6). Sew around the sole, making sure all the layers are caught in the seam.

3. Trim and notch the seam (FIGURE 7). Turn the shoe right side out.

4. Repeat Steps 1–3 to sew the remaining upper to the other sole.

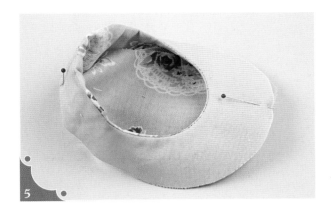

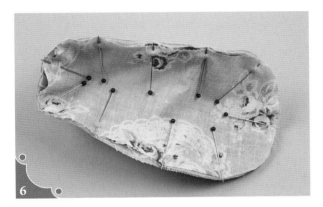

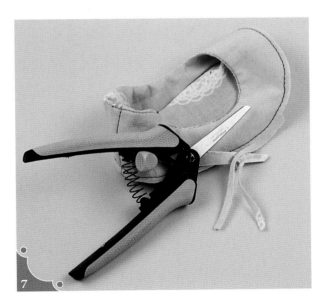

Making and Attaching the Strap

1. Fold under ¼″ on each short end of a strap piece and press. Repeat with remaining strap piece.

2. See Making a Strap (page 18) to fold and press the strap. Topstitch the strap ⅛″ along each long edge. Repeat with the second strap.

3. Separate the hook-and-loop tape pieces and place the rough side of each onto the back of the straps on opposite ends (FIGURE 8). Sew in place. See Applying Hook-and-Loop Tape (page 12).

4. Pin a strap to the inner edge of the upper (FIGURE 9). Stitch a small rectangular shape at the end of strap (or sew back and forth several times) to secure. Repeat with remaining strap and upper.

5. Place the soft side of a hook-and-loop tape piece on the outer side of a shoe so it lies under the hook-and-loop tape on the strap, as shown below. Sew in place. Repeat with other shoe.

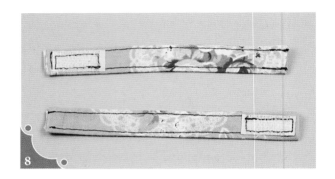

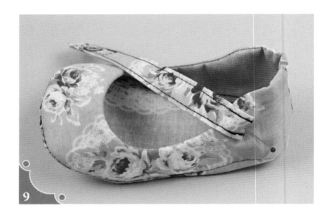

Making the Sole Lining

1. Place 2 of the sole linings right sides together and pin. Sew around the outer edge, leaving an opening on the side to turn right side out (FIGURE 10).

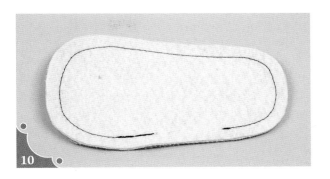

2. Notch the seam (FIGURE 11). Turn the sole lining right side out and slipstitch to close the opening or topstitch all around the sole.

3. Insert the sole lining into the shoe (FIGURE 12). Tack the shoe lining to the shoe exterior with a few hand stitches.

4. Repeat Steps 1–3 to make the other sole lining.

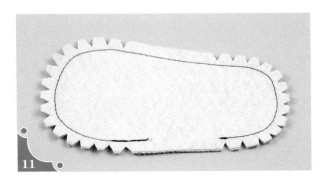

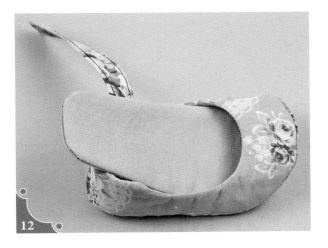

Making the Corsage

1. Fold a petal in half. Fold it in half again and insert a pin to keep it folded (FIGURE 13). Repeat to fold a total of 16 petals.

2. Choose one unfolded petal for the base. Place a folded petal on the base petal with the folded point in the center and hand stitch in place (FIGURE 14). Fold and sew 7 more folded petals to the base petal (FIGURE 15). Repeat this step to make the other corsage.

3. If you prefer, stitch a bead securely to the center of the flower using invisible thread (FIGURE 16). Attach a corsage to each shoe.

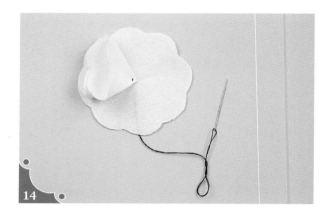

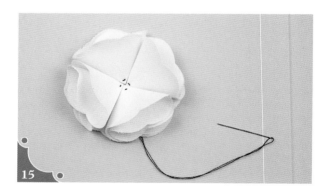

Christine Baby Mary Janes can be made with a small amount of fabric and are great for crawling babies, indoor play, and stroller trips.

Robert Baby Booties

FINISHED SIZE: U.S. baby shoe sizes 1–5 ✦ **SKILL LEVEL:** ℓℓℓ Intermediate

Not quite Mary Janes, not quite sneakers, the Robert Baby Booties are a unisex design of baby booties that are both comfortable to wear and easy to put on. The pleats make the booties more comfortable. In addition, these booties require only a tiny bit of fabric and are absolutely adorable matched with a wide range of outfits. Make Robert Baby Booties as a lovely, personal gift for your new nephew or a friend's baby daughter.

See pullout page P3 for the Robert Booties sole, upper top, upper side, lining upper, and strap patterns.

Materials

- ¼ yard 44″-wide home decor or quilting-weight cotton fabric (or 1 fat quarter) for exterior
- ¼ yard or 1 fat quarter quilting-weight cotton for lining
- ¼ yard 44″-wide fusible interfacing, such as Shape-Flex by C&T Publishing
- 2″ piece of ½″-wide hook-and-loop tape

Cutting

A ¼″ seam allowance is included in the patterns.

Trace the patterns on the wrong side of a single layer of fabric. For the pieces that require mirror-image pieces (1 and 1 reversed), use 2 layers of fabric placed right sides together.

See Drawing and Cutting the Shoe Pattern, page 15. Cut out the pattern pieces as follows.

EXTERIOR
Cut 2 upper top pieces on fold.

Cut 4 upper side pieces (2 and 2 reversed).

Cut 2 sole pieces (1 and 1 reversed).

Cut 4 strap pieces.

LINING
Cut 2 lining upper pieces on fold.

Cut 2 sole pieces (1 and 1 reversed).

INTERFACING
Cut 2 lining upper pieces on fold.

Cut 2 sole pieces (1 and 1 reversed).

Cut 2 strap pieces.

OTHER
Cut 2 pieces of hook-and-loop tape, each 1″ long.

Assembly

Use a ¼" seam allowance unless otherwise directed. Backstitch at the beginning and end of each seam.

Fusing the Interfacing

Fuse the interfacing on the wrong side of the corresponding lining pieces and exterior strap pieces, following the manufacturer's instructions.

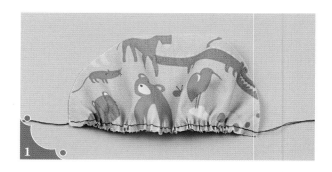

Sewing the Exterior Upper

1. Sew a running stitch (or machine basting stitch) along the edge of the upper top as marked on the pattern. Pull the thread slightly to gather (FIGURE 1).

2. Place the exterior upper side pieces on an exterior upper top piece with right sides together. Align the short end, noting the proper orientation of the angled edges. Pin and stitch (FIGURE 2).

3. Repeat Steps 1 and 2 with the remaining exterior upper and side pieces.

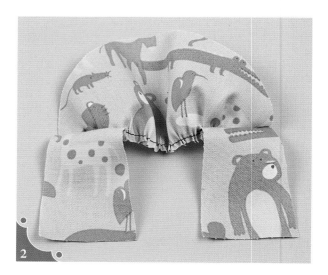

Assembling the Exterior and Lining Upper

1. Place the lining upper and exterior upper right sides together. Pull the basting thread to adjust the exterior upper to match the lining upper. Pin in place and sew the center seam, leaving 1″ unsewn on both ends. Backstitch at the beginning and end of the seam (FIGURE 3).

2. Fold the upper in half lengthwise with the lining right sides together. Pin and sew the heel seam of the lining only (FIGURE 4). Press the seam open. Do not sew the exterior heel seam.

3. Align the exterior heel edges with right sides together. Pin the exterior heel pieces (FIGURE 5) and stitch. Press the seam open.

4. Pin the exterior upper to the lining upper, aligning the exterior heel seam and the lining heel seam. Sew across the heel to complete the inner seam.

5. Clip the corners of the upper's inner seam (FIGURE 6). Turn the upper right side out and press. Topstitch ⅛″ away from the upper top gathers, if desired.

6. Repeat Steps 1–5 with remaining exterior upper and lining upper.

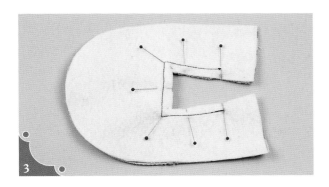

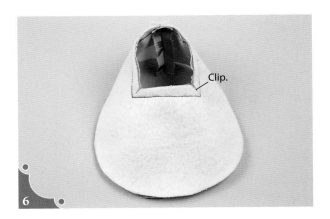

Clip.

Sewing the Strap

1. Sew a rough piece of hook-and-loop tape to the right side of a strap piece, near the curved end.

2. Pin and stitch 2 exterior strap pieces (1 with interfacing and 1 without interfacing) with right sides together, backstitching on both ends. Leave the short end open. Notch the curves (FIGURE 7).

3. Turn the strap right side out through the open end. Press and topstitch ⅛" away from the edge.

4. Pin the strap on the middle of the exterior upper top and side seam (FIGURE 8). Baste in place.

5. Repeat Steps 1–4 to make and attach the other strap to the instep of the remaining shoe.

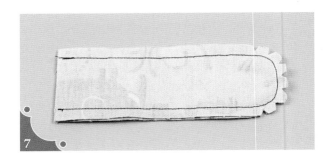

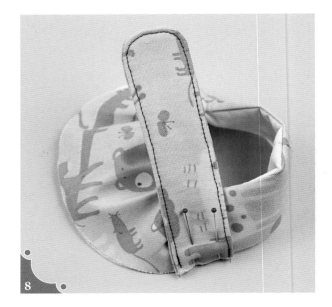

Sewing the Upper and Sole

1. Place the assembled upper on the sole lining so the upper lining is right sides together with the sole lining. Match the center points and pin the toe and heel (FIGURE 9). Be certain to pin through all layers.

2. Pin around one side of the sole, notching the heel seam as needed. Pin the rest of the sole and baste all the way around.

3. Place the exterior sole piece on the upper with right sides together, matching the center points. Pin the toe and heel first (FIGURE 10).

4. Pin around the rest of the sole, notching the heel seam allowance as needed. Sew around the sole, leaving a small opening for turning. Make sure all the layers are caught in the seam (FIGURE 11).

5. Notch the seam allowance. Turn the shoe right side out. Pin and sew the opening closed.

6. To sew the hook-and-loop piece to the upper, separate the hook-and-loop tape and sew the soft piece to the side of the exterior upper, under the end of the strap. See Applying Hook-and-Loop Tape (page 12).

7. Repeat Steps 1–6 for the other shoe.

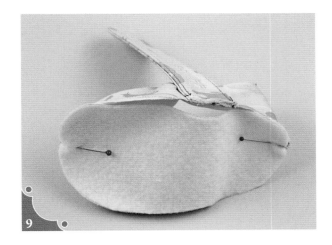

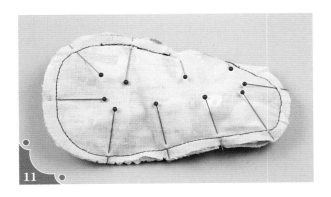

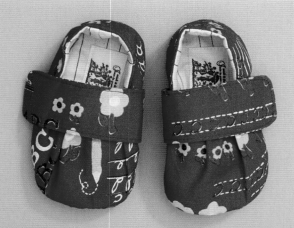

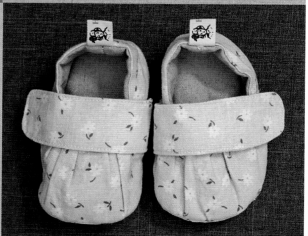

Make Robert Baby Booties as a lovely, personal gift for your new nephew or a friend's baby daughter.

Adam Elastic Baby Booties

FINISHED SIZE: U.S. baby shoe sizes 1–5 • **SKILL LEVEL:** ᘓᘓ Confident Beginner

The simple style of the Adam Elastic Baby Booties matches well with a more casual attire for both girls and boys. Because their design is so gender neutral, it is up to you to decide the overall feel of the booties with the fabric and decorations you choose. If you are making these booties for a baby girl, using a pink fabric and adding a ribbon to the center will give them an adorable, girlish look. For boys, you may decide to sew an awesome robot or Superman logo on the top. The possibilities are endless. With their elastic closure, Adam Elastic Baby Booties are easy to slip on and off. These booties are suitable for all four seasons and are great for outdoor stroller wear or indoor play, worn as an alternative to socks.

See pullout page P3 for the Adam Elastic Baby Booties upper and sole patterns.

Materials

- ¼ yard 44″-wide home decor or quilting-weight cotton fabric for exterior
- ¼ yard quilting-weight fabric for lining
- ¼ yard of 44″-wide fusible interfacing, such as Shape-Flex by C&T Publishing
- ⅔ yard of ¼″-wide elastic

Cutting

A ¼″ seam allowance is included on the patterns.

Trace the patterns on the wrong side of a single layer of fabric. For the pieces that require mirror-image pieces (1 and 1 reversed), use 2 layers of fabric placed right sides together.

See Drawing and Cutting the Shoe Pattern, page 15. Cut out the pattern pieces as follows.

EXTERIOR
Cut 2 upper pieces.

Cut 2 sole pieces (1 and 1 reversed).

LINING
Cut 2 upper pieces.

Cut 2 sole pieces (1 and 1 reversed).

INTERFACING
Cut 2 upper pieces.

Cut 2 sole pieces (1 and 1 reversed).

OTHER
Cut 2 pieces of elastic, 12″ each.

Assembly

Use a ¼" seam allowance unless otherwise directed. Backstitch at the beginning and end of each seam.

Fusing the Interfacing

Fuse the interfacing to the wrong side of the corresponding lining pieces, following the manufacturer's instructions.

Sewing the Upper

1. Fold the exterior upper pieces in half lengthwise with right sides together. Pin and sew the heel seam, backstitching at each end. Press the seam open. Repeat with remaining exterior upper piece. Sew the lining upper pieces in the same manner (FIGURE 1).

2. Turn the exterior upper right side out. Place the lining upper on the exterior upper with right sides together and pin (FIGURE 2). Stitch around the inner seam.

3. Notch the curved seams (FIGURE 3). Turn the piece right side out.

4. Press and topstitch ⅛" from the inner edge, starting and ending at the heel point. Backstitch 3–4 times at the start and end. Then pin and sew another row of stitching in the same manner ½" from the inner edge to create a casing for the elastic (FIGURE 4).

5. Repeat Steps 2–4 for the other upper.

Exterior

Lining

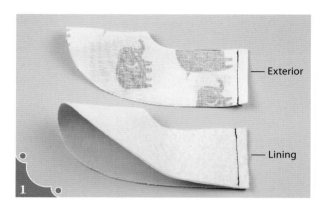

Sewing the Upper and Sole

1. Place the upper piece and the sole lining together so the upper lining faces the right side of the sole lining and the center points match. Pin the toe and heel. Pin around about half of the sole, notching the heel seam allowance as needed. Then pin around the rest of the sole (FIGURE 5). Baste all around the sole. Be certain all layers are included.

2. Place the exterior sole piece right sides together with the exterior upper piece, matching their center points. Pin the toe and heel first (FIGURE 6).

3. Pin around the rest of the sole, notching the heel seam as needed. Sew around the sole, leaving a small opening for turning. Make sure all the layers are caught in the seam. Notch the seam. Turn the bootie right side out through the opening. Pin and sew the opening closed.

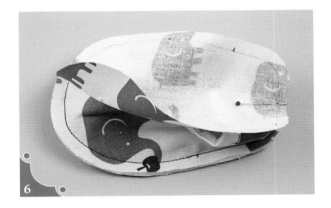

4. Snip a few stitches at the top of the exterior's heel seam between the 2 rows of stitching for the elastic channel. Attach a small safety pin to an end of a length of elastic. Feed the elastic through the channel (FIGURE 7), taking care not to twist the elastic. Gather the inner edge as desired, overlap the ends of the elastic, and stitch back and forth across to secure. Push the elastic back into the channel. Cut off the excess elastic. Sew the heel seam closed with a few hand stitches.

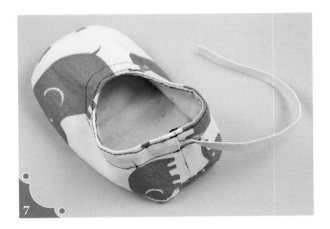

5. Repeat Steps 1–4 for the other bootie.

These booties are suitable for all four seasons and are great for outdoor stroller wear or indoor play, worn as an alternative to socks.

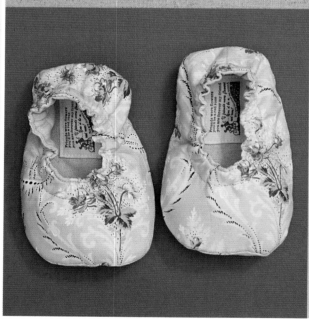

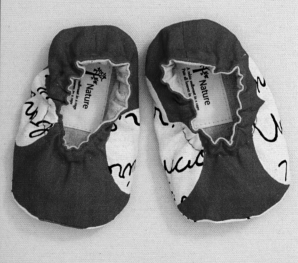

Isaac Baby Boots

FINISHED SIZE: U.S. baby shoe sizes 1–5 ◆ **SKILL LEVEL:** Beginner

The Isaac Baby Boots are a style with a fuzzy, warm, furry lining.
Simple to make and cute to wear, these boots are a must-have for your baby boy or girl during the colder months. They can be made entirely by hand sewing; in fact, it is easier to make them by hand than with a sewing machine. The visible faux fur lining is this boot's key feature, providing softness suitable for your baby's sensitive skin. Pamper your little one with the Isaac Baby Boots. •◦•◦•◦•

See pullout page P3 for the Isaac Baby Boots upper, shaft front, shaft back, and sole patterns.

Materials

· ⅓ yard 44″-wide home decor or quilting-weight cotton fabric for exterior

· ⅓ yard 44″-wide faux fur, plush, fleece, or microfiber fabric for lining

· 6″ piece of ½″-wide hook-and-loop tape

· 8 buttons ½″ wide

Cutting

A ¼″ seam allowance is included in the patterns.

Trace the patterns on the wrong side of a single layer of fabric. For the pieces that require mirror-image pieces (1 and 1 reversed), use 2 layers of fabric placed right sides together.

See Drawing and Cutting the Shoe Pattern, page 15. Cut out the pattern pieces as follows.

EXTERIOR
Cut 2 upper pieces.

Cut 2 shaft front pieces (1 and 1 reversed).

Cut 2 shaft back pieces (1 and 1 reversed).

Cut 2 sole pieces (1 and 1 reversed).

LINING
Cut 2 upper pieces.

Cut 2 shaft front pieces (1 and 1 reversed).

Cut 2 shaft back pieces (1 and 1 reversed).

Cut 2 sole pieces (1 and 1 reversed).

Assembly

Use a ¼" seam allowance unless otherwise directed. Backstitch at the beginning and end of each seam.

Sewing the Upper

1. Fold an exterior upper piece in half lengthwise with right sides together. Pin and sew along the straight heel seam (FIGURE 1). Press the seam open.

2. Place the exterior upper on an exterior sole with right sides together. Pin the toe and heel first. Pin around the rest of the seam. Notch the curved seam allowance as needed.

3. Sew the exterior upper to the sole. Notch the curved seam (FIGURE 2).

4. Repeat Steps 1–3 to assemble the remaining exterior upper and sole. Sew the lining upper and sole pieces in the same manner. Trim the lining seams.

5. Turn the assembled exterior upper/sole right side out. Tuck the assembled lining upper/sole into the assembled exterior upper/sole with wrong sides together (FIGURE 3). Baste the top opening of the upper pieces together. Repeat for the other boot.

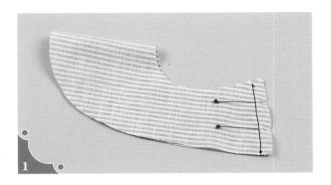

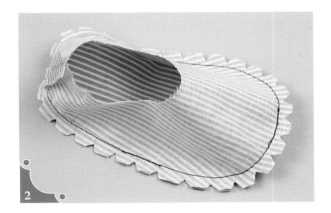

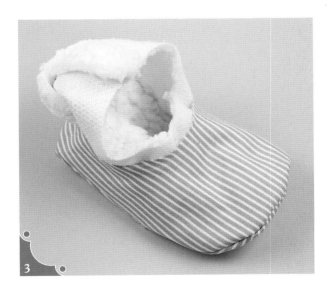

Making the Shaft

1. Place an exterior shaft back piece on an exterior shaft front piece with right sides together. Match Point A and Point B and pin in place. Be sure the pieces are aligned as shown (FIGURE 4). Stitch along the side seam. Press the seam open. Repeat for the other exterior shaft front and back, as well as the lining shaft pieces.

2. Attach the rough side of the hook-and-loop tape to the right side of the lining shaft front as indicated on the pattern. See Applying Hook-and-Loop Tape (page 12). Attach the other rough piece to the remaining lining shaft front in the same manner.

3. Pin the exterior shaft to the lining shaft with right sides together. Sew along the top and side seams (FIGURE 5). Notch the curved seams. Turn right side out. Sew the shaft pieces for the other boot in the same manner.

4. The shaft with the back piece on the left side is for the left boot (FIGURE 6).

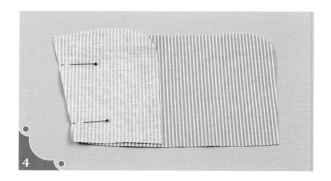

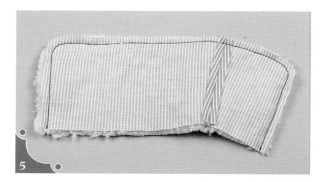

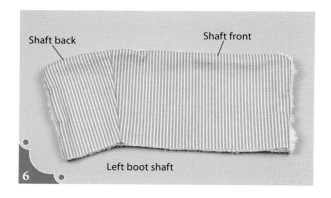

Shaft back   Shaft front

Left boot shaft

Assembling the Upper and Shaft

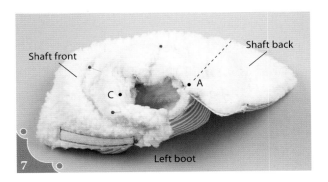

1. Place the assembled shaft on the upper with the exterior right sides together. The lining shaft will be right side up. Pin the upper Point A and assembled shaft Point A first. Match Point C on the upper to Point C on the shaft front. Pin the shaft front first and then pin the shaft back (FIGURE 7).

2. The shaft back will overlap the shaft front a little bit (FIGURE 8). Stitch the shaft to the upper. Use an overlock or zigzag stitch to finish the seam. Flip the shaft up so the exterior is right side up.

3. Sew the soft side of the hook-and-loop piece on the exterior shaft back. See Applying Hook-and-Loop Tape (page 12).

4. Attach 4 buttons to the side where the shaft front overlaps the shaft back, sewing through all layers of the shaft front to secure.

5. Repeat Steps 1–4 for the other boot.

Baby Hats and Bibs

Veronica Hat

FINISHED SIZE *(approximate head circumference):*
S: 16½″ (3 months) ✦ *M:* 17½″ (6 months) ✦ *L:* 18½″ (12 months) ✦ *XL:* 19″ (18 months)
SKILL LEVEL: ll Confident Beginner

The Veronica Hat is an easy sewing project that will get lots of use. Completed in a little over an hour using little fabric, it makes an excellent present for your own children as well as for those of relatives and friends. The wide brim keeps your little one's head cool and ensures that your child gets the protection she needs while playing outside in the sun.

The Veronica Hat can also be made for boys by adding cotton straps and snaps, as done with the cute little safari hat (page 64). For the girls, a corsage is a nice addition to the hat. The Veronica Hat makes for a fashionable finish to any outfit and goes well with a wide range of styles.

See pullout page P3 for the Veronica Hat top, band, and brim patterns.

Materials

- ½ yard home decor or quilting-weight cotton fabric for exterior
- ½ yard lightweight fabric for lining
- ½ yard 44″-wide lightweight fusible interfacing for apparel (such as Shape-Flex by C&T Publishing)
- 1 yard cotton string for straps (*optional*)
- 1 wooden bead for straps (*optional*)

Cutting

A ⅜″ seam allowance is included in the pattern pieces.

Trace the patterns on the wrong side of a single layer of fabric. Cut out the pieces from the exterior, lining, and interfacing as follows.

EXTERIOR
Cut 1 top piece.

Cut 1 band piece on fold.

Cut 1 brim piece on fold.

LINING
Cut 1 top piece.

Cut 1 band piece on fold.

Cut 1 brim piece on fold.

INTERFACING
Cut 1 top piece.

Cut 1 band piece on fold.

Cut 1 brim piece on fold.

COTTON STRING (*optional*)
Cut 2 pieces of string, 18″ each.

Assembly

Use a ⅜" seam allowance unless otherwise directed.
Backstitch at the beginning and end of each seam.

Fusing the Interfacing

Fuse the interfacing to the wrong side of the corresponding lining pieces, following the manufacturer's instructions.

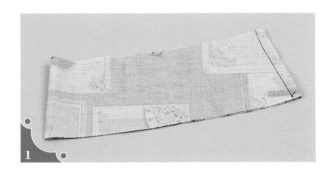

Sewing the Band and Top

1. Fold the exterior band piece in half with right sides together. Pin the short ends together and stitch (FIGURE 1). Press the seam open.

2. Pin the inner edge of the exterior band piece to the exterior top piece with right sides together. Pin the 4 points first as marked on the pattern. Sew around the circle. Notch the seam allowance (FIGURE 2).

3. Repeat Steps 1 and 2 to assemble the lining band and top. Leave a 2½"–3" opening in the seam to allow for turning.

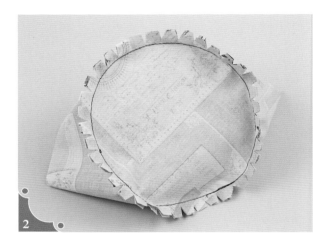

Making the Brim

1. Fold the exterior brim piece in half with right sides together. Pin and sew the short ends together. Sew the lining brim piece in the same manner (FIGURE 3). Press the seams open.

2. Place the exterior brim and lining brim pieces right sides together. Pin in place and sew along the outer curved seam. Notch the seam (FIGURE 4).

3. Turn the assembled brim right side out and press. Topstitch ⅛″ from the outer edge. Add 3 more rows of stitching spaced approximately ¾″ apart (FIGURE 5).

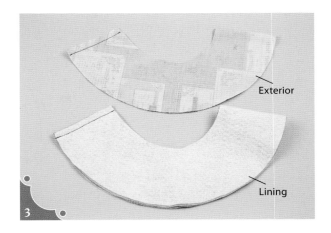

Exterior

Lining

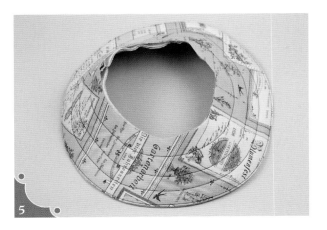

Assembling the Brim and Lining

1. Align the bottom edge of the band with the inner edge of the brim so the exterior band and exterior brim pieces are right sides together. Pin (FIGURE 6) and baste in place. If you would like to add the ties, attach a piece of string to either side of the hat (FIGURE 7).

2. Tuck the assembled hat from Step 1 into the lining band/top with right sides together, sandwiching the brim between the exterior and lining. Align the bands, pin, and stitch (FIGURE 8).

3. Turn the hat right side out through the lining opening. Pin and sew the opening closed. If you added ties, insert both loose ends through a wooden bead and knot the ends of the inserted strings together.

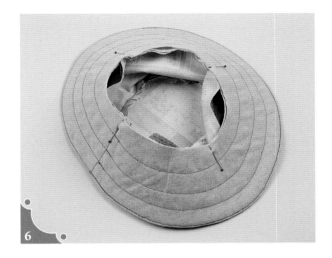

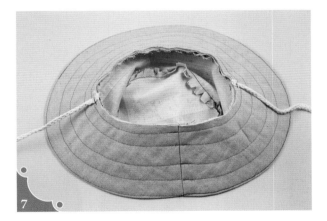

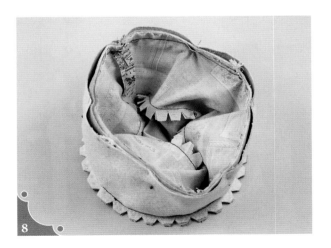

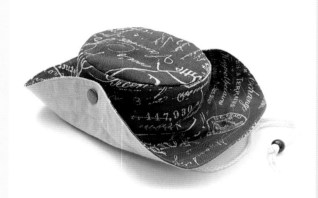

The Veronica Hat makes for a fashionable finish to any outfit and goes well with a wide range of styles.

Deliah Pixie Hat

FINISHED SIZE (*approximate head circumference*):
S: 16½″ (3 months) ✦ **M:** 17½″ (6 months) ✦ **L:** 18½″ (12 months) ✦ **XL:** 19″ (18 months)
SKILL LEVEL: ℓ Beginner

Ever imagined a pixie hat for babies? The Deliah Pixie Hat is just that! Designed for beginners, the Deliah Hat is appealing to all levels of sewists. For the best results, carefully choose your exterior and lining fabrics first. Then, consider the color of the bias tape since it can make the hat even more eye-catching. Adding a corsage to the hat for the girls will also spice up the finished project.

Linen, eyelet, and wool are all possible materials to consider for this hat. Even if you're not an experienced sewist, the outcome will still be that of a professional. So start your Deliah Pixie Hat today!

See pullout page P4 for the Deliah Pixie Hat pattern.

Materials

- ½ yard or 2 fat quarters 44″-wide quilting-weight cotton or linen/cotton fabric for exterior
- ½ yard or 2 fat quarters lightweight fabric for lining
- ½ yard of 44″-wide lightweight fusible interfacing, such as Shape-Flex by C&T Publishing, for apparel (*optional*)
- 1 sewing label (*optional*)
- 1⅔ yards (or 60″) of ⅜″-wide double-fold bias tape*

* *See Making Bias Strips (page 14) to make your own.*

Cutting

A ⅜″ seam allowance is included on the pattern.

Trace the pattern directly onto the wrong side of a single layer of fabric as shown, and then flip it over and draw it again to create 1 and 1 reversed.

EXTERIOR
Cut 2 hat pieces (1 and 1 reversed).

LINING
Cut 2 hat pieces (1 and 1 reversed).

INTERFACING (*optional*)
Cut 2 hat pieces (1 and 1 reversed).

BIAS TAPE
Cut a 16″ piece for the neck edge.

Cut a 36″ piece for the front edge and ties (*recommended length*).

Assembly

Use a ⅜″ seam allowance unless otherwise directed.
Backstitch at the beginning and end of each seam.

1. If desired, fuse interfacing to the wrong side of the lining pieces, following the manufacturer's instructions.

2. Fold an exterior hat piece along the center of the dart. Pin and sew along the dart (FIGURE 1). Repeat with the other exterior hat piece.

3. Place the exterior hat pieces right sides together. Fold the darts so they lie in opposite directions (FIGURE 2).

4. Pin and sew along the top and back. Notch the seams (FIGURE 3).

5. Repeat Steps 2–4 with the lining hat pieces.

6. Turn the exterior hat right side out.

Dart

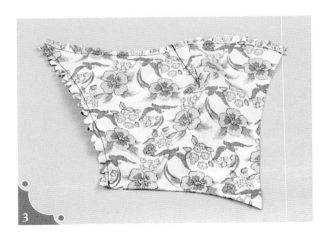

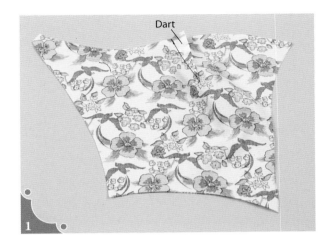

6. Place the lining inside the exterior with wrong sides together (FIGURE 4).

7. Baste the raw edges of the exterior and lining together around the face and neck.

8. To make a pleat, bring the fold line to meet the placement line (as indicated on the pattern) and pin in place. Make 2 pleats on each side of the back seam. Baste across the pleats, close to the edge (FIGURE 5).

Attaching the Bias Tape

1. Fold the tape over the neck edge of the hat and pin in place (FIGURE 6). Stitch ⅛″ away from the edge of the bias tape. Trim any excess bias tape at either end.

2. Wrap the front edge bias tape over the front edge of the hat, matching the midpoint of the bias tape to the top center seam. Pin in place (FIGURE 7).

3. Trim the ties to the desired length. Fold the short end of each tie under ¼″ and press (FIGURE 8). Refold the bias tape and press again.

4. Starting at the end of a tie, stitch along the bias tape ⅛″ away from the open edge. Stitch along the tie, around the face, and to the end of the other tie, backstitching at both ends.

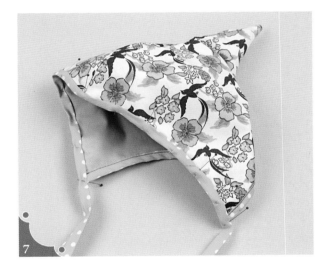

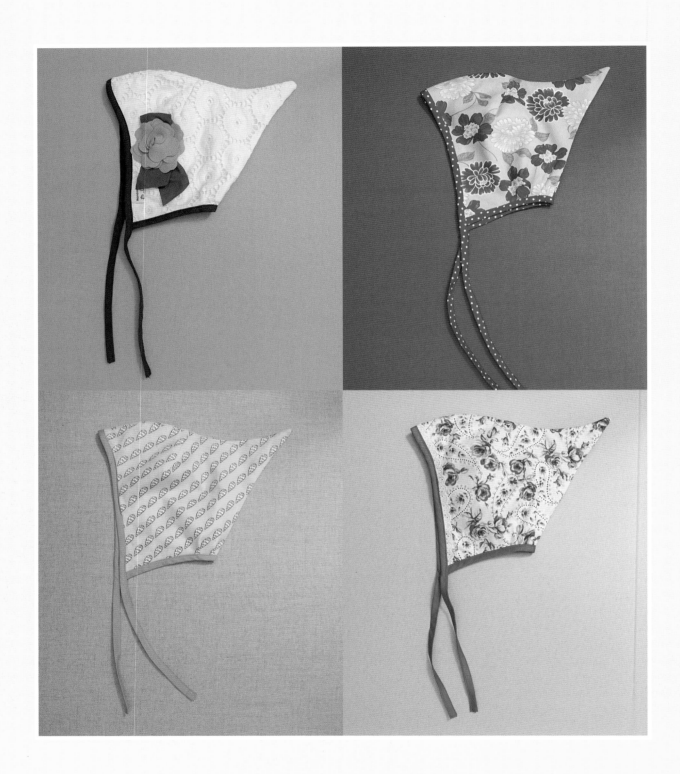

Baby Boutique

Abigail Baby Bib

FINISHED SIZE: approximately 9¼″ × 14½″ (when snapped) ◆ **SKILL LEVEL:** ℓ Beginner

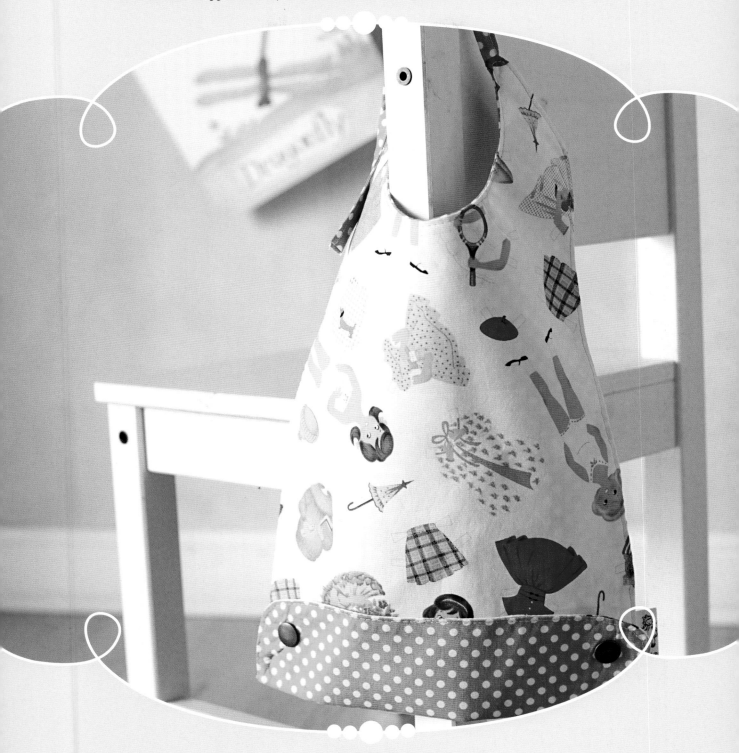

Simple and easy to make, the Abigail Baby Bib pattern is very accessible to beginners. The bib is designed with snaps along the lower edge so when snapped together it forms a little pouch to catch all the food the baby misses. For easy cleanup, make the bib using waterproof fabric or an iron-on vinyl. The Abigail Bib will be a very welcome, practical gift. The key to this project is choosing coordinating fabric for the lining and exterior because the lining will become visible when snapped. Ribbons are a nice, quick alternative to fabric ties.

See pullout page P4 for the Abigail Baby Bib pattern.

Materials

- ½ yard 44″-wide home decor fabric or laminate/oilcloth for exterior
- ½ yard lightweight cotton fabric for lining and straps
- 2 snaps
- 1 sewing label (*optional*)

Cutting

A ⅜″ seam allowance is included on the pattern.

Join the bib upper and lower patterns to make 1 pattern. Place the pattern on folded fabric and trace. Cut out pieces as follows.

EXTERIOR
Cut 1 bib piece on fold.

LINING
Cut 1 bib piece on fold.

Cut 2 strap pieces 1½″ × 12½″.

Making the Straps

1. Press under ¼″ at a short end of a strap piece.

2. Follow the instructions in Making a Strap (page 18) to fold and press the strap.

3. Topstitch ⅛″ away from the long open edge of the strap.

4. Repeat Steps 1–3 with the remaining strap.

5. Baste the short raw ends of the straps to the exterior bib piece as indicated on the pattern (FIGURE 1). Loosely tie the straps to keep them out of the way when stitching the bib.

Assembly

Use a ⅜″ seam allowance unless otherwise directed. Backstitch at the beginning and end of each seam.

Assembling the Exterior and Lining

1. Place the lining on the exterior with right sides together. The straps should be sandwiched between the 2 pieces. Pin and sew together, leaving a 5″ opening at the bottom for turning. Stitch several times over the straps. Notch the curved seams (FIGURE 2).

2. Turn the bib right side out through the opening and press. Topstitch ¼″ away from the edge (FIGURE 3).

3. Follow the manufacturer's instructions to attach snaps where indicated on the pattern. If you are using a snap that will show when closed, be sure to attach the snap as if the lining were the outside of the garment, so that the top of the snap shows when snapped (FIGURE 4).

April Baby Bib

FINISHED SIZE: 9¼" × 5½" • **SKILL LEVEL:** Beginner

A tiny bib that is easy for sewists of all experience levels,
the April Baby Bib distinguishes itself from the rest with its unique bias at the neck. Additionally, the bib has a pacifier holder, which will ensure that the baby doesn't lose it this time around! The pacifier snaps to a strap so it is easy to remove for washing. Carefully selecting the fabric colors for the bib and ties will determine the look of the project. Since the bib is easy to make, sewing one for each day of the week would be a welcome and practical gift.

See pullout page P1 for the April Baby Bib pattern.

Materials

- ¼ yard or 1 fat quarter 44″-wide quilting-weight cotton fabric for exterior
- ¼ yard or 1 fat quarter 44″-wide quilting-weight cotton fabric for lining
- 1½ yards of ⅜″-wide double-fold bias tape*
- 1 small snap
- 1 sewing label (*optional*)

* See Making Bias Strips (page 14) to make your own.

Cutting

A ⅜″ seam allowance is included in the pattern.

Draw the pattern directly onto the wrong side of folded fabric; then cut as follows.

EXTERIOR
Cut 1 bib piece on fold.

LINING
Cut 1 bib piece on fold.

DOUBLE-FOLD BIAS TAPE
Cut 1 piece 32″ for neck edge and ties.

Cut 1 piece 9″ for pacifier strap.

Assembly

Use a ⅜″ seam allowance unless otherwise directed. Backstitch at the beginning and end of each seam.

Making the Pacifier Strap

1. Unfold the 9″ pacifier strap and fold a short end under ¼″. Refold and press.

2. Topstitch ⅛″ away from the long edge to close the strap.

3. Baste the raw end of the pacifier strap to the exterior bib piece as indicated on the pattern (FIGURE 1).

Assembling the Exterior and Lining

1. Place the bib lining onto the bib exterior with right sides together. The pacifier strap should be sandwiched between the 2 pieces. Pin and stitch along the shoulder and bottom. Backstitch over the strap several times. Leave the neck edge unstitched (FIGURE 2). Notch the curves.

2. Turn the bib right side out. Press and topstitch ¼″ away from the edge, leaving the neck open (FIGURE 3).

3. Open each end of the 32″ bias tape, turn under ¼″, and press. Refold the ends and press.

4. Insert the neck of the bib into the bias tape, matching the midpoint of the tape to the midpoint of the bib neck. Pin in place (FIGURE 4). Topstitch from one end of the bias tape to the other end.

5. Following the manufacturer's instructions, attach half of the snap to the end of the pacifier strap. Attach the other half of the snap 2½″ above.

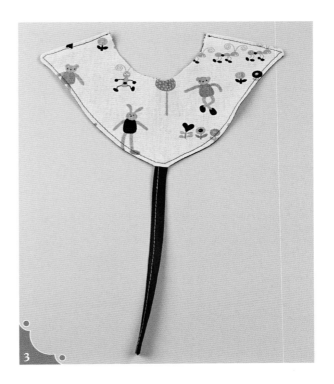

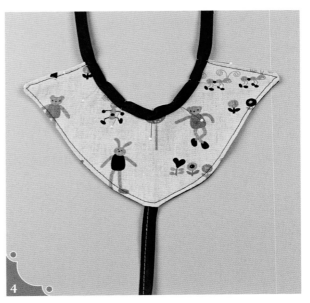

Baby Boutique

Toys

Isabella Doll

FINISHED SIZE: approximately 13″ tall ◆ **SKILL LEVEL:** Confident Beginner

The Isabella Doll is the perfect gift for a girl who wants a cute little friend! The hair is made with felt, making the pattern easy and accessible for beginners. It is possible to add hair ornaments depending on the kind of hairstyle you make for the doll. Parts of the doll's body are made using a print fabric, so the doll is fully dressed when the skirt is added. In addition, the body and legs are one pattern, resulting in a pattern that is simpler than traditional ones.

See pullout page P1 for the Isabella Doll body, arm, head/eye, hair top, hair right, and hair left patterns.

Materials

- ¼ yard or 1 fat quarter 44″-wide quilting-weight cotton print fabric for body and skirt
- ⅛ yard or 1 fat quarter 44″-wide quilting-weight cotton for pantaloons
- ¼ yard or 1 fat quarter 44″-wide muslin fabric for face, hands, and legs
- 11″ × 2″ fabric for shoes
- 12″ × 9″ felt piece for hair
- 2″ × 1″ felt scrap for eyes
- 9″ piece ¼″-wide elastic for skirt
- Small pearls for hair ornament (*optional*)
- 12″ lace for pantaloons (*optional*)
- Nontoxic fabric glue for attaching the eyes (*optional*)
- Embroidery thread for the eyes
- Fiberfill

Cutting

A ¼″ seam allowance is included on the patterns.

Draw the patterns directly onto the wrong side of a single layer of fabric. Body and arm pieces are traced after piecing strips together.

PRINT DRESS FABRIC

Cut 1 strip 11″ × 4½″ for body.

Cut 1 strip 9″ × 3½″ for arms.

Cut 1 piece 15″ × 5½″ for skirt.

PANTALOONS

Cut 1 strip 11″ × 3¾″ for pantaloons.

MUSLIN

Cut 1 head piece for face.

Cut 1 strip 11″ × 1″ for legs.

Cut 1 strip 9″ × 2¼″ for hands.

FELT

Cut 2 hair top pieces.

Cut 1 hair right piece.

Cut 1 hair left piece.

Cut 1 head piece for head back.

BLACK FELT (*optional*)

Cut 2 circles ⅜″-wide for eyes (as shown on head pattern).

SHOES

Cut 1 strip 11″ × 2″.

Assembly

Use a ¼″ seam allowance unless otherwise directed.
Backstitch at the beginning and end of each seam.

Making the Head

1. Place the hair right piece on the face, as indicated on the head pattern. Pin and topstitch in place (FIGURE 1).

2. Lay the hair left piece on the face as shown. Pin and topstitch in place (FIGURE 2).

3. Place the 2 hair top pieces right sides together. Sew around the top, leaving the bottom edge open. Notch the seam (FIGURE 3).

4. Turn the hair top right side out and stuff with a little bit of fiberfill (FIGURE 4). Topstitch ¼″ and ½″ from the upper edge.

5. Center the hair top on the top of the head. Baste in place (FIGURE 5).

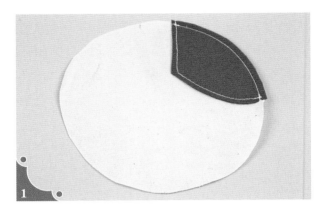

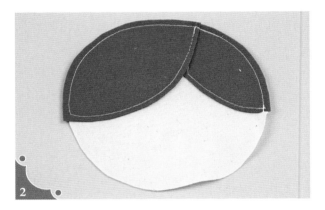

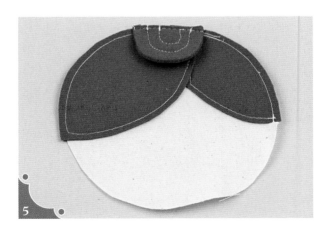

Sewing the Arm and Hand

1. Place the 9″ × 3½″ strip of dress fabric and the 9″ × 2¼″ strip of muslin right sides together. Pin the long edge and stitch. Press the seam open.

2. Fold the fabric from Step 1 in half with right sides together. Place the arm pattern on the wrong side, aligning the dashed line on the pattern with the seam in the fabric. Trace the arm pattern twice on the folded fabric; then cut. You will have 4 arm pieces (2 and 2 reversed).

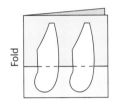

Trace arm pattern twice on folded fabric.

3. Place 2 arm pieces right sides together. Pin and sew around the arm, leaving the top open for turning. Notch the seam. Repeat with remaining arm pieces (FIGURE 6).

4. Turn 1 arm right side out and fill with fiberfill (FIGURE 7). Repeat with the other arm.

Sewing the Body Pieces

1. Sew the 11″ strips (body print, pantaloons, leg, and shoe strips) together along the 11″ edges, as shown (FIGURE 8). Press seams open. Add lace on the right side of the pantaloons/leg seam before assembling, if desired.

2. Fold the fabric from Step 1 in half with right sides together. Trace around the body pattern on the wrong side of the folded fabric, aligning the dashed lines as with the arms (FIGURE 9). Cut out the doll body.

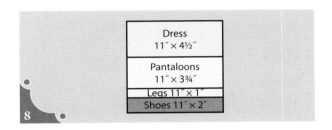

| Dress 11″ × 4½″ |
| Pantaloons 11″ × 3¾″ |
| Legs 11″ × 1″ |
| Shoes 11″ × 2″ |

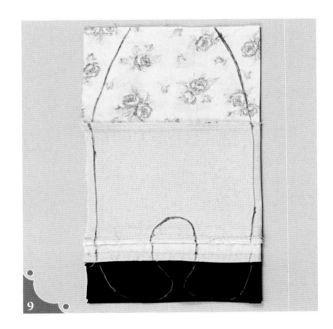

3. Place the face piece on a body piece, aligning the neck edges, with right sides together. Pin and sew along the neck edge. Start and stop sewing ¼″ from each end and backstitch on both ends of the seam (FIGURE 10). Press the seam open. Assemble the head back and remaining body piece in the same manner.

4. Place the arms on the doll front piece as indicated on the pattern. Baste the arms in place (FIGURE 11).

5. Place the doll back on the doll front with right sides together. The hair top and arms will be sandwiched between the 2 layers. Pin and sew all around the body with a small stitch length, leaving a gap for turning (FIGURE 12).

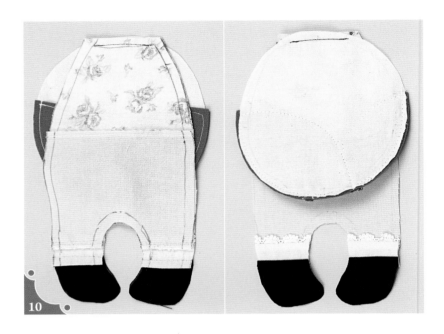

6. Notch the seam well. Turn the doll right side out and stuff with fiberfill (FIGURE 13).

7. Sew the opening closed.

8. Attach the eyes using glue or by hand sewing.

Making the Dress

1. Fold the skirt piece in half with right sides together. Pin and sew along the short ends. Press the seam open.

2. To make the elastic casing, fold under ½″ at the top of the skirt and press. Fold the top edge under ½″ again and press. Pin and topstitch close to the edge, leaving a 1″ opening to insert the elastic. See Making the Casing for Elastic (page 19).

3. To sew the hem, fold the bottom edge under ¼″ twice, press, and topstitch (FIGURE 14).

4. Attach a small safety pin to an end of the elastic and insert into the casing opening. Pull the elastic through the casing, gathering the skirt. Try the skirt on the doll and adjust the elastic to fit. Overlap the ends of the elastic and stitch across the overlap several times. Cut off any excess elastic. Stitch the casing opening closed.

5. Place the skirt onto the doll's waist.

The Isabella Doll is the perfect gift for a girl who wants a cute little friend!

Teddy Bear

FINISHED SIZE: approximately 16″ tall ✦ **SKILL LEVEL:** Beginner

This is a very easy pattern that can be made with terry cloth or jersey fabric.
For those of us who are not used to sewing with plush, the bear can be made entirely by hand sewing. However, there is no need to worry if hand sewing is not your forte! Due to the fluffy nature of the plush material, when the doll is completed, the sewing line will not show, effectively hiding the hand-stitched lines. After completing the doll, I recommend adding a finishing touch such as a muffler or scarf made from ribbons or fabric scraps.

See pullout page P2 for the body, head, arm, leg, and ear patterns.

Materials

- ½ yard 44″-wide plush, terry cloth, knit, fleece, or felt for body, arms, legs, ears, and head
- Embroidery floss for nose and eyes
- Fiberfill
- Fabric scrap for scarf (*optional*)

Cutting

A ¼″ seam allowance is included on the patterns.

Fold ½ yard of fabric in half with right sides together, aligning the selvage edges. Draw the patterns directly onto the wrong side of the double layer of fabric. Trace the head and body* patterns once each and cut to get 2 pieces (1 and 1 reversed). Trace the arm, leg, and ear* patterns each twice and then cut to get 4 pieces of each (2 and 2 reversed).

* The ear and body pieces are symmetrical, so the patterns don't need to be reversed, but it saves time to cut them from 2 layers of fabric with right sides together, along with the other pieces.

BODY FABRIC
Cut 2 body pieces.

Cut 2 head pieces (1 and 1 reversed).

Cut 4 ear pieces.

Cut 4 arm pieces (2 and 2 reversed).

Cut 4 leg pieces (2 and 2 reversed).

Assembly

Use a ¼˝ seam allowance unless otherwise directed. Backstitch at the beginning and end of each seam.

Sewing the Arms, Legs, and Ears

1. Align 2 arm pieces (1 and 1 reversed) with right sides together. Pin and stitch around the arm. Leave the top open for turning. Stitch the other arm pieces in the same manner.

2. Stitch the leg pieces and ear pieces in the same manner (**FIGURE 1**).

3. Trim the arm seam allowance. Turn right side out through the opening using a turning tool or capped pen; then stuff with fiberfill. Repeat this process for other arm and leg pieces. It is not necessary to fill the ears with fiberfill.

Sewing the Body

1. Fold a body piece in half with right sides together as shown (**FIGURE 2**). Stitch the darts at the top and bottom. Sew the darts on the remaining body piece in the same manner.

2. Position the arms on the right side of a body piece as indicated on the pattern. Baste in place (**FIGURE 3**).

3. Baste the legs in place in the same manner (**FIGURE 4**).

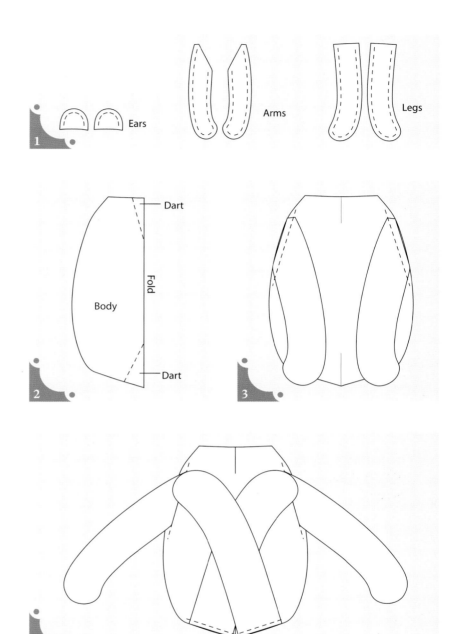

4. Place the remaining body piece on top of the piece from Step 3 with right sides together. Pin and sew around the body, leaving the neck open for turning (FIGURE 5).

5. Notch and trim the seam well. Turn right side out (FIGURE 6). Stuff the body with fiberfill.

Making the Head

1. Place an ear on the right side of a head piece as indicated on the pattern. Pin and baste in place (FIGURE 7). Attach the other ear to the remaining head piece in the same manner.

2. Fold a head piece in half with right sides together, aligning the sides of the V at the top, and pin. Stitch along this edge, making certain to catch the raw edge of the ear in the seam (FIGURE 8). Sew the other head piece in the same manner.

3. Place the head pieces together with right sides facing. Pin and stitch, leaving the bottom neck edge open for turning. Notch the seam.

4. Turn the head right side out (FIGURE 9) and stuff with fiberfill.

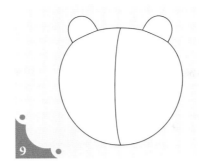

Attaching the Head and Body

1. Fold the neck openings of the body and head under ¼" and pin together. Use a slip-stitch to join the head to the body (FIGURE 10). Add a little fiberfill to the neck area before completing the stitching, if needed.

2. Sew the nose in a triangular shape with a satin stitch using 6 strands of embroidery floss. Stitch the eyes in the same manner (FIGURE 11).

3. Cut the scarf fabric in a long strip or a triangle and tie it around the neck, if you wish.

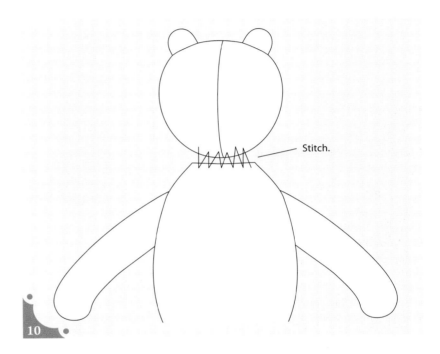

Stitch.

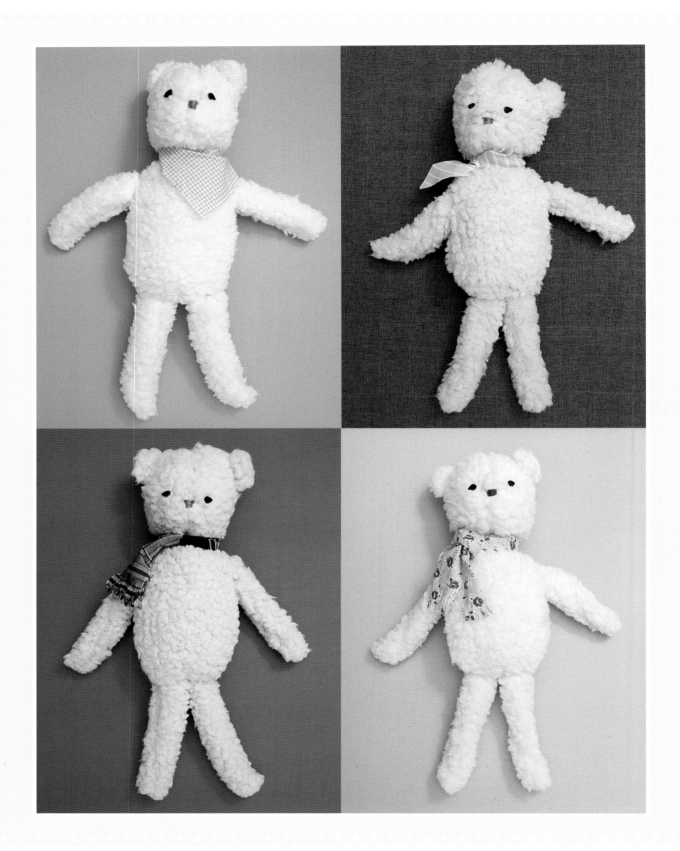

Animal Rattles and Neck Rest

FINISHED SIZES: *Bird:* approximately 5½″ × 4″ • *Giraffe:* approximately 6″ × 7″
Elephant: approximately 5¼″ × 3¼″ • *Neck Rest:* approximately 5″ × 6″ • **SKILL LEVEL:** ℒ Beginner

This rattle set includes various shapes that babies can hold, play with, and enjoy. The bird rattle includes a separate wing, which adds another dimension and gives it a cute look. Choosing the right colors to contrast the wing and the bird body will make this rattle even more eye-catching. Adding ribbons to the tail of the bird or the neck of the giraffe is a nice finishing touch. The rattles can also be made into a baby mobile by attaching strings to the rattles. The rattle noisemaker can easily be purchased at a local dollar store. Although a rattle can be made using one piece of fabric, you can also patch fabric together before cutting the pattern. The neck rest makes a fun rattle on its own, or make it in coordinating fabrics to create a cute gift set.

See pullout pages P1 and P2 for the Rattles bird head front, bird wing, bird body front, bird back, giraffe, elephant, and neck rest patterns.

Materials

- ¼ yard or 1 fat quarter 44"-wide quilting-weight cotton or linen/cotton fabric
- ¼ yard of ½"-wide ribbon (optional)
- 1 or 2 rattle noisemakers
- Fiberfill

Cutting

A ¼" seam allowance is included in the patterns.

Trace the patterns on the wrong side of a single layer of fabric. For the pieces that require mirror-image pieces (1 and 1 reversed), use 2 layers of fabric placed right sides together. Cut out the pattern pieces as follows.

BIRD

Cut 1 head front piece.

Cut 1 body front piece.

Cut 1 back piece.

Cut 2 wing pieces (1 and 1 reversed).

ELEPHANT

Cut 2 elephant pieces (1 and 1 reversed).

GIRAFFE

Cut 2 giraffe pieces (1 and 1 reversed).

Assembly

Use a ¼″ seam allowance unless otherwise directed. Backstitch at the beginning and end of each seam.

Sewing the Bird Wing

1. Place the wing pieces right sides together. Pin and stitch around the outer edge, leaving the inside edge open for turning (FIGURE 1). Notch the seam allowance or use pinking shears.

2. Turn the wing right side out and press. Insert a little bit of fiberfill (FIGURE 2).

3. Topstitch 2 lines (FIGURE 3) as indicated on the pattern.

Sewing the Body Front

1. Place the wing onto the body front piece and baste in place (FIGURE 4).

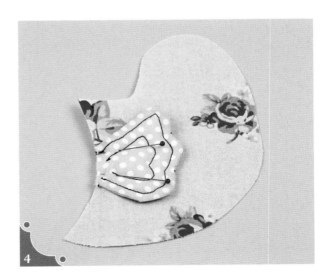

2. Place the bird head front piece on the body front piece with right sides together. Pin together, notching the seam allowance, if needed. Stitch, then notch the seam (FIGURE 5).

3. Press the seam allowance toward the head front and topstitch ⅛″ away from the seam (FIGURE 6).

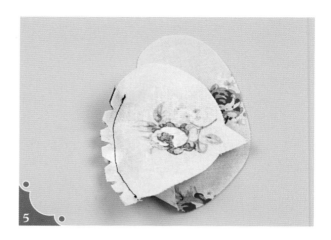

Adding Ribbons

To add a tactile element to your rattles, insert pieces of ribbon into the seams.

Fold a piece of ribbon in half with wrong sides together. Place the folded ribbon on the edge of the assembled  bird front and baste in place. Then continue to assemble and stuff the rattle as directed.

Cut 3 pieces of ribbon, each 1½″ long, for the giraffe. Fold the ribbons in half with wrong sides together and baste to the neck edge before sewing the front to the back.

Sewing and Stuffing the Body

1. Place the front and back pieces with right sides together. Pin and sew around the edge, leaving an opening for turning (FIGURE 7). Notch the seam allowance. Turn right side out and press.

2. Stuff fiberfill in the body. Insert 1 or 2 rattle noisemakers in the body. Close the opening securely.

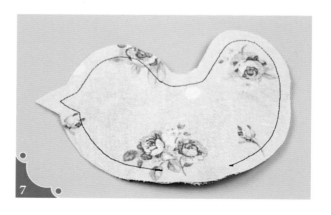

● ● ELEPHANT OR GIRAFFE ● ●

To make the elephant or giraffe rattles, follow Steps 1 and 2 of Sewing and Stuffing the Body (above).

Animal Rattles and Neck Rest

Neck Rest

In addition to the animal rattles, you can easily make a C-shaped or neck rest rattle. This shape is easy for babies to hold and makes a great neck rest for the Teddy Bear (page 89).

Materials

¼ yard or 1 fat quarter 44″-wide quilting-weight cotton fabric for exterior

1 or 2 rattle noisemakers

Fiberfill

Cutting

Cut 2 pieces on the fold.

To make the neck rest rattle, follow Steps 1 and 2 of Sewing and Stuffing the Body (page 98).

Diaper Bags, Pouch, and Quilt/Blanket

Rhoda Boston Diaper Bag

FINISHED SIZE: 19½″ × 14¼″ × 5″ ◆ **SKILL LEVEL:** Intermediate

The sizable, roomy, and convenient Rhoda Boston Diaper Bag is perfect when going on long trips and vacations. The elastic pockets on the inside of the bag keep items secure. An added key holder on a strap allows mothers to find their keys without having to hunt around in their bag while holding the baby. The outside pockets provide even more space, which is always needed. With both a long strap and handles, the bag can be carried over the shoulder or by hand. ●●●●●

See pullout page P1 for the Rhoda Boston Diaper Bag upper curve and lower curve patterns.

Materials

- 2 yards 44″-wide home decor or quilting-weight cotton fabric or laminate for exterior
- 2 yards lightweight cotton fabric for lining
- 1 yard of 44″-wide heavyweight fusible interfacing
- ½ yard of 44″-wide lightweight fusible interfacing (such as Shape-Flex by C&T Publishing) for outer pocket
- 1 all-purpose 24″ zipper
- 1⅓ yards of ¼″-wide elastic for lining pockets
- 4½ yards of ½″-wide double-fold bias tape for binding seams*
- 4½ yards piping* (*optional*)
- 2½″-wide O-ring for shoulder strap
- Lobster clasp with a ½″ opening for key holder

* See Making Bias Strips (page 14) and Making and Attaching Piping (page 16). For this project, we made the bias tape from the lining fabric and the piping using a solid green fabric.

Cutting

A ½″ seam allowance is included in all cutting measurements.

EXTERIOR

Cut 2 pieces 20½″ × 15¼″ for exterior front and back.

Cut 2 pieces 20½″ × 9¾″ for the outer pocket.

Cut 1 piece 20½″ × 2″ for outer pocket binding.

Cut 2 zipper panels 3″ × 25″.

Cut 2 pieces 6″ × 21″ for the gusset.

Cut 2 pieces 4″ × 16½″ for the handles.

Cut 1 piece 6″ × 20″ for the shoulder strap loop.

Cut 1 piece 6″ × 38″ for the shoulder strap.

LINING

Cut 2 pieces 20½″ × 15¼″ for the lining front and back.

Cut 2 pieces 3″ × 25″ for zipper panels.

Cut 2 pieces 6″ × 21″ for the gusset.

Cut 2 pieces 30½″ × 10½″ for the inner pockets.

Cut 1 piece 12″ × 1¾″ for the key holder.

BIAS TAPE

Cut 2 pieces of bias tape 6″ long for the gusset.

Cut 2 pieces 67″ for interior seam binding.

INTERFACING

Cut 2 pieces 20½″ × 15¼″ for the front and back.

Cut 2 pieces 25″ × 3″ for the zipper panels.

Cut 2 pieces 21″ × 6″ for the gusset.

Cut 1 piece 20½″ × 9¾″ for the outer pocket.

OTHER

Cut 2 elastic pieces 22″ long for the inner pockets.

Assembly

Use a ½" seam allowance unless otherwise directed.
Backstitch at the beginning and end of each seam.

Preparing the Pieces

1. Fuse the corresponding interfacing pieces to the wrong side of the following lining pieces: front, back, zipper panels, and gusset pieces. Fuse interfacing to 1 outer pocket piece as well.

2. Neatly stack the exterior front, exterior back, lining front, and lining back pieces. Pin the pieces together to keep them aligned. Measure ⅝" from the top right corner and mark the top edge. Measure 2" up from the bottom right corner and mark the side. From the lower right mark to the top right mark, cut through all 4 layers. In similar fashion, mark and trim the left side (FIGURE 1).

3. Trace the Rhoda upper curve pattern in the upper right corner of the stack. Flip the upper curve pattern and trace it in the upper left corner. Trace the lower curve pattern in the lower right corner, flip, and trace it in the lower left corner (FIGURE 2). Cut along the drawn curves to round the corners of all 4 layers. Unpin the layers and set aside.

4. Stack the 2 outer pocket pieces and pin to keep aligned. Repeat Step 2 (above), measuring ⅜" in from each of the top corners and 2" above each of the bottom corners. Cut through both layers as shown (FIGURE 3).

5. Trace the lower curve pattern in the lower right corner, flip the pattern, and trace it in the lower left corner (FIGURE 4). Cut the lower curves. Leave the upper corners of the outer pocket pieces as is.

6. Repeat Step 5 to trace and cut the 2 lower curves of the inner pocket pieces. Leave the upper corners of the inner pocket pieces as is.

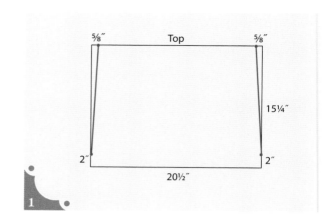

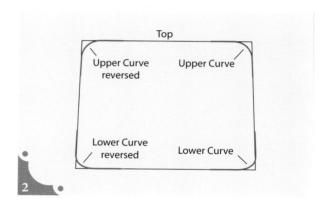

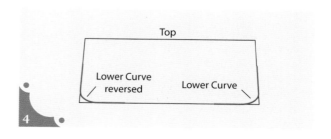

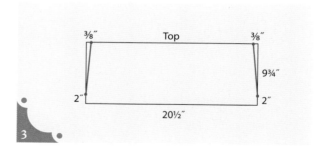

Making the Outer Pocket

1. Fold the outer pocket binding strip in half lengthwise with wrong sides together and press. Open the fold, bring each side to the middle, and press. Refold the initial fold and press.

2. Place the outer pocket pieces wrong sides together.

3. Wrap the binding around the top edge of outer pocket pieces. Pin and sew ⅛″ away from the folded edge of the bias tape (FIGURE 5).

4. Lay the assembled outer pocket on the exterior front piece. Pin and sew the pocket's center divider line, stitching several times over the pocket binding to secure. Baste the pocket to the exterior front along the bottom and sides (FIGURE 7).

Sewing the Handle and Straps

1. Make the 2 handles using the 4″ × 16½″ pieces. Fold each long edge under ½″ and press. Fold the handle in half lengthwise with wrong sides together and press. Topstitch along each long edge of the handle (FIGURE 6). Repeat to fold and topstitch the remaining handle and the 6″ × 20″ shoulder strap loop piece.

2. Center a handle on the top edge of the right side of the front exterior. The front exterior is the piece with the outer pocket. The handle ends should be placed 2¼″ from the center point (FIGURE 7). Pin and baste the handle in place. Repeat this process to baste the other handle to the back exterior piece.

3. Insert one end of the shoulder strap loop piece through the O-ring and fold the loop piece in half.

4. To make the shoulder strap, fold one short end under ½″. Fold each long edge under ½″ and press. Fold in half lengthwise and topstitch along each long edge and the folded short end.

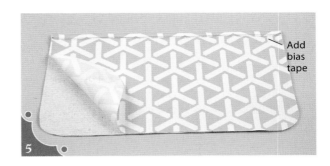

Add bias tape

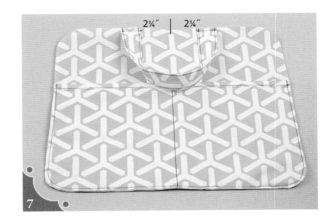

2¼″ | 2¼″

5. Stitch the exterior gusset pieces together end to end. Press the seam open.

6. Center the loop piece on one end of the gusset and baste in place. Center the raw edge of the shoulder strap on the other end of the gusset and baste in place (FIGURE 8).

7. If you would like to have a key holder, fold a short end of the 12″ × 1¾″ piece under ¼″, press, and follow the instructions in Making a Strap (page 18). Topstitch along the long edge to close. Insert the folded short end through the base of the lobster clasp and stitch to secure (FIGURE 9). Set aside.

Sewing the Zipper

1. Place the zipper on 1 exterior zipper panel with right sides together. Trim the zipper if necessary, leaving ½″ at each end.

2. Pin the zipper in place. Stitch close to the outer edge of the zipper tape using a zipper foot (FIGURE 10).

3. Place 1 lining zipper panel piece right side down on the back of the zipper. The right side of the lining piece should be facing the right side of the exterior piece.

4. Pin the lining panel and zipper together. The zipper will now be between the exterior zipper panel and lining zipper panel. Sew the lining close to the zipper teeth (FIGURE 11).

5. Press the lining and exterior panels away from the zipper with wrong sides together. Topstitch along the edge of the zipper panel near the zipper.

6. Repeat Steps 1–5 to attach the remaining exterior and lining zipper panels to the other side of the zipper (FIGURE 12).

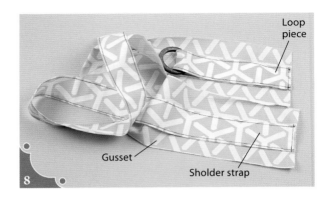

Loop piece

Gusset

Sholder strap

8

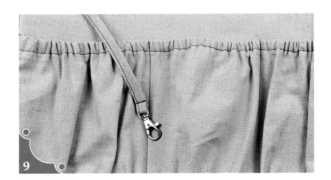

9

10

11

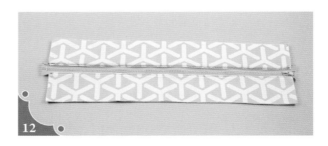

12

Sewing the Zipper Panel and Gusset

1. Sew the 2 lining gusset pieces together end to end to make 1 piece. Press the seam open.

2. Pin and baste the lining gusset piece and exterior gusset piece together with *wrong* sides facing.

3. Place the assembled zipper panel on the gusset with the exterior right sides together. The strap should be sandwiched between the 2 pieces. Pin and sew the short ends so the zipper panel and gusset form a circle (FIGURE 13). Trim the seam allowances slightly.

4. Fold a 6″ piece of bias tape over a seam allowance from Step 3, encasing the seam allowance. Pin and sew ⅛″ away from the edge of the bias tape (FIGURE 14). Repeat to add bias tape to the remaining gusset seam allowance.

Making the Lining

1. To make a casing for elastic at the top of an inner pocket, fold the top edge under ½″ to the wrong side and press. Fold over another ½″ and press. Follow Steps 2–5 of Making the Casing for Elastic (page 19) to gather the top edge of the pocket (FIGURE 15).

2. With a long stitch length, sew ¼″ from the bottom edge of the inner pocket piece. Pull the threads to gather the bottom edge (FIGURE 16).

3. Place the lining pocket piece on the right side of the lining front piece.

4. Stitch the left end of the elastic to the left edge of the lining; then pull the elastic out to the desired length and sew the right end of the elastic in place. The elastic should lie flat, not too tight or too loose. Trim excess elastic.

13

14

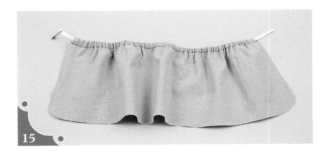

15

16

Rhoda Boston Diaper Bag

5. Adjust the gathers at the bottom of the pocket to align the bottom and sides of the pocket and lining. Pin and baste the pocket in place along the bottom and sides.

6. Sew vertical lines to divide the pocket as desired (FIGURE 17).

7. Repeat Steps 1–6 with the remaining inner pocket and lining back piece.

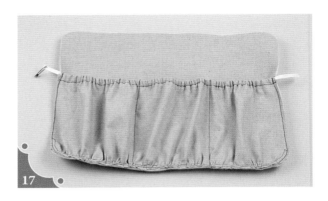

Assembling the Exterior and Lining

1. Pin and baste the exterior front and lining front pieces together with *wrong* sides facing.

2. Pin and baste the exterior back and lining back pieces together with *wrong* sides facing. Pin the key holder to the top left corner of the lining back and baste in place. Refer to Figure 20 (page 109) for placement guidance.

3. If you would like to add piping, pin and baste it around the edge of the exterior front and back pieces. See Making and Attaching Piping (page 16).

4. Pin the front piece to the assembled zipper panel and gusset with exterior right sides together. Center the zipper panel along the top edge of the front piece; then pin the rest of the gusset around the edge. Clip the corners of the front piece to fit, if necessary.

5. Sew the front and gusset together (FIGURE 18). Open the zipper.

6. Repeat Steps 3–5 to attach the back to the gusset.

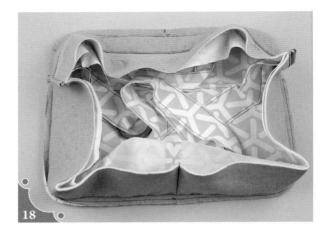

Binding the Inside

1. Unfold a 67″ piece of bias tape and pin it, with right sides together, to the seam that joins the bag front and gusset. Align the raw edges. To join the ends, fold an end under ¼″ and pin (FIGURE 19). Lay the other end on top of the folded end, overlapping about 1″.

2. Stitch 1 edge of the bias tape in place.

3. Refold the bias tape, encasing the seam allowance. Topstitch close to the edge of the bias tape (FIGURE 20).

4. Repeat Steps 1–3 to attach the remaining 67″ bias tape to the bag back and gusset seam.

5. Turn the bag right side out. Loop the free end of the shoulder strap through the O ring. Adjust the strap to the desired length and stitch to secure (FIGURE 21).

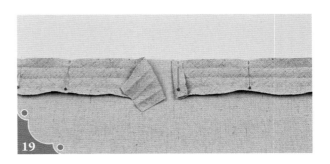

19

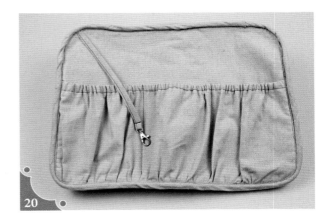

20

21

Rhoda Boston Diaper Bag

With both a long strap and handles, the bag can be carried over the shoulder or by hand.

Doreen Diaper Bag

FINISHED SIZE: 17″ × 12″ × 4″ (not including handles) ✦ **SKILL LEVEL:** Confident Beginner

The Doreen Diaper Bag was designed for mothers who go on short visits. The numerous lining pockets in the bag give it more room than would appear. Two additional pockets on the sides of the bag are ideal for baby bottles, and the pleats give the bag room to expand. You can make the bag using one fabric or add a coordinating fabric for the handles. This bag is the perfect size for carrying over your shoulder while holding the baby—not too big and not too small. Although the bag may seem difficult to make, it's fairly easy when taken one section at a time.

See pullout page P4 for the Doreen Diaper Bag handle and bag patterns.

Materials

- 1½ yards 44″-wide home decor or quilting-weight cotton fabric for exterior
- 1½ yards quilting-weight fabric for lining
- 1½ yards 44″-wide fusible interfacing (such as Shape-Flex by C&T Publishing)
- 1 magnetic snap
- 2 yards elastic for exterior side and lining pockets

Cutting

A ½″ seam allowance is included on the patterns.

Join the Handle A and Handle B patterns to create 1 handle pattern. Draw the patterns on folded fabric, as indicated. Cut the exterior, lining, and interfacing as follows.

EXTERIOR

Cut 2 bag pieces on the fold.

Cut 2 handle pieces on the fold.

Cut 2 pieces 5″ × 11¾″ for the sides.

Cut 2 pieces 7″ × 9¼″ for the outer side pockets.

Cut 1 piece 18″ × 5″ for the bottom.

LINING

Cut 2 bag pieces on the fold.

Cut 2 handle pieces on the fold.

Cut 2 pieces 5″ × 11¾″ for the sides.

Cut 1 piece 18″ × 5″ for the bottom.

Cut 2 pieces 27″ × 7½″ for the inner pockets.

INTERFACING

Cut 2 bag pieces on the fold.

Cut 2 handle pieces on the fold.

Cut 2 pieces 5″ × 11¾″ for the sides.

Cut 1 piece 18″ × 5″ for the bottom.

ELASTIC

Cut 2 pieces of elastic 6″ long for outer side pockets.

Cut 2 pieces of elastic 22″ long for lining pockets.

Assembly

Use a ½" seam allowance unless otherwise directed. Backstitch at the beginning and end of each seam.

Fusing the Interfacing

Fuse the interfacing to the wrong side of the corresponding lining pieces following the manufacturer's instructions.

Making the Exterior Pockets and Lining Pockets

1. Follow Steps 1–7 of Making the Lining in the Rhoda Boston Diaper Bag (pages 107 and 108) to gather (FIGURE 1) and attach the inner pockets to the lower bag lining pieces.

2. Follow Steps 1–7 of Making the Lining in the Rhoda Boston Diaper Bag to gather the side pockets and attach to exterior side pieces (FIGURE 2).

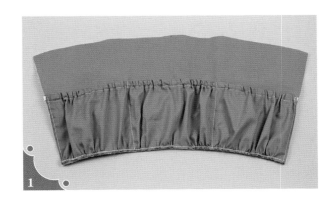

Attaching the Magnetic Snap

Following the manufacturer's instructions, attach the magnetic snaps to the right side of the lining handle pieces where indicated on the handle pattern (FIGURE 3).

Making the Exterior and Lining

1. Fold the pleats on an exterior bag piece as indicated on the pattern, bringing the fold lines to meet the placement lines. Pin in place. The pleats should face the center of the bag (FIGURE 4). Baste the pleats in place near the top edge.

2. Place an exterior bag piece on an exterior handle piece with right sides together. Pin and stitch (FIGURE 5). Notch the seam allowance.

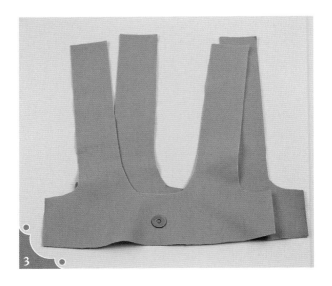

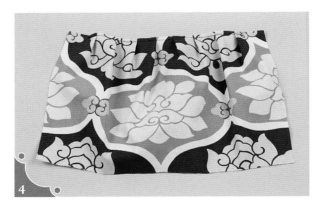

3. Press the seam toward the handle. Topstitch on the right side of the handle piece, ⅛″ away from the seam (FIGURE 6).

4. Repeat Steps 1–3 with the remaining exterior handle and bag. Repeat Steps 1–3 with the lining bag and lining handle pieces as well.

5. Pin an exterior side piece to the left edge of the exterior bag front with right sides together. The outer pocket should be sandwiched between the 2 layers. Pin the other side piece to the right edge of the exterior bag front (FIGURE 7).

6. Stitch, leaving the first and last ½″ unsewn. Be sure to backstitch at either end of these seams.

7. Pin the exterior bag back to the sides in the same manner (FIGURE 8). Stitch, leaving the first and last ½″ unsewn.

8. Pin the exterior bottom to the assembled exterior (FIGURE 9). Stitch all 4 sides, pivoting at the corners.

9. Trim the corners.

10. Repeat Steps 5–9 (pages 115 and 116) to assemble the lining pieces. Leave a 5″ opening at the lower edge for turning (FIGURE 10).

Assembling the Exterior and Lining

1. Turn the exterior right side out and tuck it into the lining with right sides together (FIGURE 11).

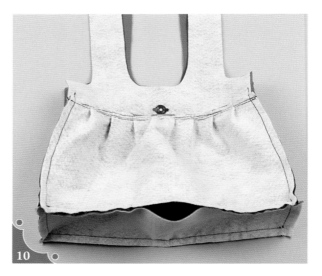

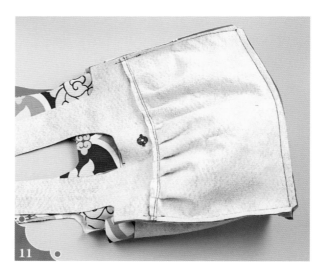

2. Pin and sew the exterior front and lining front from Point A on one handle to Point A on the other handle, as shown. Pin from Point B to Point C on each side and stitch as shown (FIGURE 12). Stitch the exterior back and lining back in the same manner.

3. Pin the top edge of an exterior side piece to the top of a lining side piece and stitch from Point C on the front to Point C on the back (FIGURE 13). Sew the other side in the same manner.

4. Trim the corners. Notch the curved seams (FIGURE 14).

5. Turn the bag right side out through the lining opening. Sew the opening closed. Tuck the lining into the exterior.

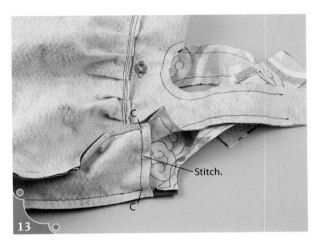

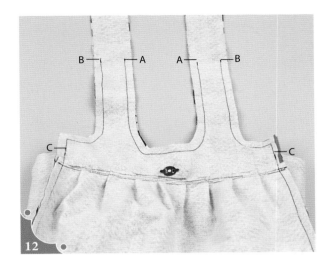

Doreen Diaper Bag

Sewing the Handles

1. Pin the short ends of the exterior front handle with right sides together. Pin the short ends of the front handle lining with right sides together as well (FIGURE 15). Repeat for the back handle exterior and lining.

2. Stitch the exterior handle ends together. Stitch the lining handle ends together. Press the seams open (FIGURE 16).

3. Fold the raw edges of the handle exterior and lining under ½″ and press (FIGURE 17). Pin the exterior handle to the lining handle (FIGURE 18).

4. Repeat Steps 1–3 with the other handle.

5. Topstitch around the armholes, the outline of the bag, and across the top of the side panel, as shown (FIGURE 19).

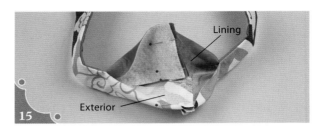

This bag is the perfect size for carrying over your shoulder while holding the baby. The numerous pockets in the bag give it more room than would appear.

Doreen Diaper Bag

Eva Pouch

FINISHED SIZE: 9″ × 10½″ ◆ **SKILL LEVEL:** ℓ Beginner

The drawstring at the top of the pouch makes it easy to open and close. The key to creating this project successfully is to coordinate the top casing and pouch body fabrics.

The Eva Pouch is very versatile. Baby shoes, hats, and toys can all be wrapped inside this pouch and presented as a gift. The pouch is also useful as a diaper bag due to its handy size.

See pullout page P1 for the Eva Pouch lower corner curve pattern.

Materials

- ¼ yard or 1 fat quarter quilting-weight cotton or home decor fabric for exterior
- ⅛ yard quilting-weight cotton or home decor fabric for casing
- ¼ yard or 1 fat quarter quilting-weight fabric for lining
- 25″ cotton string
- 1 wooden bead

Cutting

A ¼″ seam allowance is included in the cutting measurements.

EXTERIOR
Cut 2 pieces 9½″ × 10″ for the exterior front and back.

CASING
Cut 2 pieces 9½″ × 2½″ for the casing.

LINING
Cut 2 pieces 9½″ × 10″ for the lining front and back.

Eva Pouch

Assembly

Use a ¼″ seam allowance unless otherwise directed. Backstitch at the beginning and end of each seam.

Rounding the Lower Corners

1. Stack the lining front and back pieces with a 9½″ edge at the bottom. Place the exterior front and back on top of the lining pieces, aligning the edges (FIGURE 1). Pin together to keep the pieces aligned.

2. Trace the Eva Pouch lower corner curve pattern in the lower right corner of the stack. Flip the pattern and trace the curve in the lower left corner (FIGURE 2). Trim the curves, cutting through all 4 layers.

3. Transfer the dart markings on the lower curve pattern to the wrong side of each piece.

Sewing the Casing and Darts

1. Place a casing piece on the top edge of the exterior front piece with right sides together. Pin and sew along the top edge. Press the seam allowance toward the casing. Repeat with the exterior back and remaining casing.

2. Fold an exterior front dart down the middle with right sides together. Pin and sew the dart. Stitch the other dart in the same manner. Press the darts toward the center (FIGURE 3). Sew the exterior back darts in the same manner, but press the back dart seams outward. Repeat to make the lining darts.

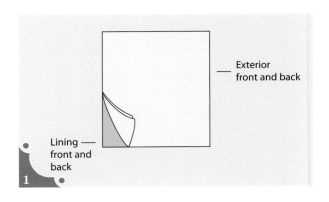

Exterior front and back

Lining front and back

1

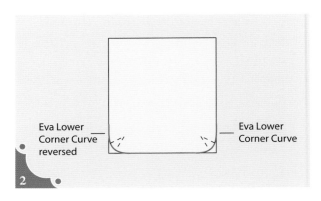

Eva Lower Corner Curve reversed

Eva Lower Corner Curve

2

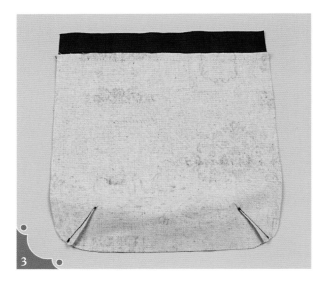

3

Sewing the Exterior and Lining

1. Pin and sew the exterior front to the exterior back with right sides together, joining the sides and bottom (FIGURE 4). Sew the lining front and back pieces in the same manner, leaving a 3½″ opening on 1 side for turning.

2. Turn the assembled exterior right side out. Tuck the exterior into the lining (FIGURE 5), with right sides facing.

3. Pin and sew the exterior to the lining around the top edge (FIGURE 6).

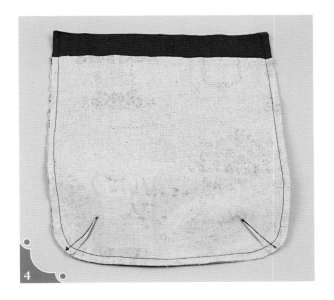

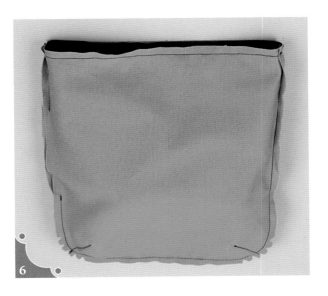

4. Turn the pouch right side out through the opening in the lining. Sew the opening closed. Tuck the lining deeply into the exterior so the casing folds in half. Half of the casing will be visible from the exterior while the other half faces the inside of the bag.

5. Press and topstitch ⅛″ from the top edge. Backstitch 3–4 times over the side seams.

6. Press the casing again. Topstitch ⅛″ from the lower edge of the casing (FIGURE 7). Backstitch 3–4 times over the side seams.

7. Carefully snip the stitches of one side seam of the casing to create an opening for the string.

8. Attach a small safety pin to one end of the string and insert into the casing opening (FIGURE 8). Work the safety pin around the top of the bag and back through the opening, gathering the casing. Insert both ends of the string through the wooden bead and knot the ends of the string together.

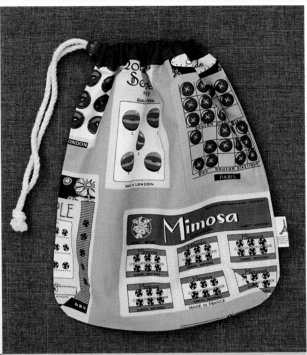

Eva Pouch

James Baby Blanket

FINISHED SIZES: *Patchwork Quilt:* 48″ × 48″ ✦ *Receiving Blanket (with optional ruffle):* 39½″ × 39½″

SKILL LEVEL: ℓ Beginner

This project has two size options: a larger patchwork blanket and a smaller receiving blanket. The receiving blanket has a hood, allowing the baby to be wrapped head to toe. A ruffle can be added to the receiving blanket, if desired. The patchwork blanket is relatively large, which makes it a gift that can be used for a long time. Consider making a patchwork blanket and a receiving blanket as a matching set!

See pullout page P4 for the James Baby Blanket hood piece pattern.

Patchwork Blanket Materials

- 36 squares 6½″ × 6½″ from various cotton print fabrics
- 1¼ yards 44″-wide solid cotton fabric for border
- 1⅔ yards 60″-wide fleece or microfiber fabric for backing
- 5½ yards piping*

* See Making and Attaching Piping (page 16) to make your own piping.

Receiving Blanket Materials

- 1⅛ yards 44″-wide quilting-weight cotton fabric for top
- ¾ yard 44″-wide quilting-weight cotton fabric for ruffle (*optional*)
- 1⅓ yards of 60″-wide fleece or microfiber fabric for backing and hood piece

Cutting

A ¼″ seam allowance is included in the pattern and cutting measurements.

PATCHWORK BLANKET CUTTING

Cotton

Cut 36 squares 6½″ × 6½″ from various fabrics.

Cut 5 border strips 6½″ × width of fabric.

Fleece

Cut 1 piece 48½″ × 48½″ for the back.

RECEIVING BLANKET CUTTING

Cotton

Cut 1 piece 35½″ × 35½″ for the top.

Cut 7 strips 3″ × width of fabric for the ruffle (*optional*).

Fleece

Cut 1 piece 35½″ × 35½″ for the back.

Cut 1 hood piece.

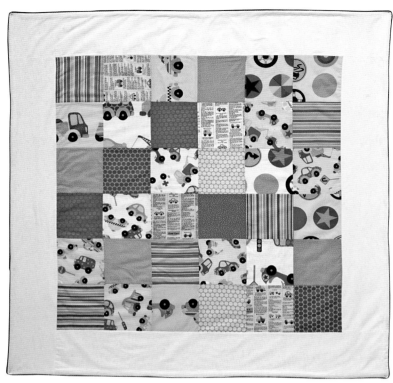

James patchwork blanket

Assembly

Use a ¼″ seam allowance unless otherwise directed.

Sewing the Patchwork

1. Place a 6½″ square on another 6½″ square with right sides together. Pin and sew along one side (FIGURE 1).

2. Press the seam open (FIGURE 2).

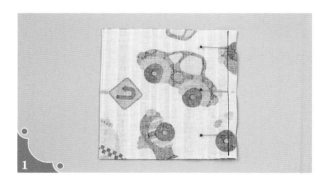

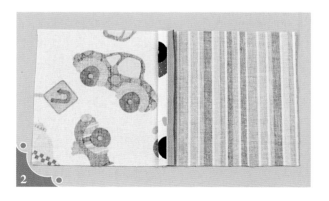

3. Repeat Steps 1 and 2 to join 6 squares to make a row. Make 6 rows of 6 squares (FIGURE 3).

4. Stitch the rows together and press the seams open (FIGURE 4).

Adding Borders and Piping

1. Measure across the center of the patchwork. Cut 2 border strips to match this measurement. Place a border strip along the top seam of the patchwork, right sides together. Pin and stitch along the top edge (FIGURE 5). Press the seam open. Repeat to add the other trimmed border strip to the bottom of the patchwork.

2. Sew the remaining 3 border strips end to end to make 1 long strip. Measure the center of the quilt top from top to bottom, including the borders. Cut 2 strips from the long border strip to match this measurement.

3. Add a border strip from Step 2 to each side of the quilt top.

4. Place the raw edge of the piping along the outer edge of the right side of the quilt top. Pin and baste the piping in place (FIGURE 6). See Making and Attaching Piping (page 16).

5. See Steps 1–4 in Assembling the Blanket (page 131) to finish the blanket.

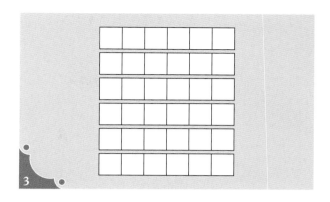

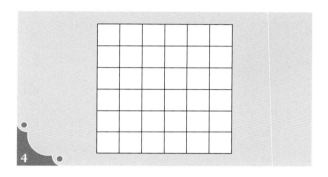

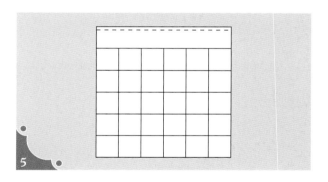

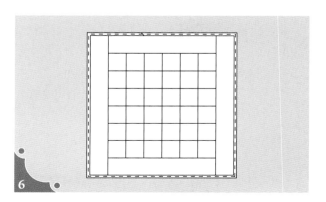

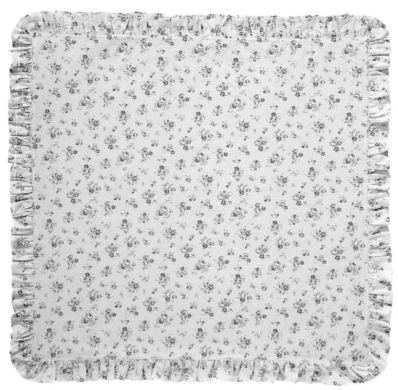

James Ruffled Receiving Blanket

• • • • • • • • • • • RECEIVING BLANKET • • • • • • • • • •

Assembly

Use a ¼″ seam allowance unless otherwise directed.

Adding the Optional Ruffle

1. To make the ruffle, sew 7 strips 3″ × width of fabric together end to end. Finish a single long edge of the joined strips using a rolled hem stitch. If your sewing machine doesn't have this option, fold the long edge under a scant ¼″ and press. Fold under a scant ¼″ again, press, and topstitch.

2. Gather the long raw edge of the strip from Step 1 using a gathering foot (or sew a long basting stitch and pull the bobbin thread to gather). Gather the ruffle until it is approximately 140″ long. Place the short ends of the ruffle right sides together, pin, and stitch.

3. With right sides together, pin the ruffle around the sides of the top, adjusting the gathers to fit. Baste in place (FIGURE 7).

Attaching the Hood

1. Fold the hood piece under twice along the diagonal as indicated on the pattern. Pin and topstitch along the fold (FIGURE 8).

2. Place the hood piece on one corner of the backing with the right side of both pieces facing up. Align the raw edges and baste in place on 2 sides of the corner (FIGURE 9).

Assembling the Blanket

1. Place the top on the backing with right sides together. The piping or ruffle should be sandwiched between the 2 layers. Pin and stitch around all 4 sides, using a ¼″ seam allowance. Leave an 8″ opening to turn right side out (FIGURE 10).

2. Trim the corners. Turn right side out.

3. Tuck in the seam allowance along the opening. Press and topstitch ⅛″ inside the edge.

4. Quilt, if desired (FIGURE 11).

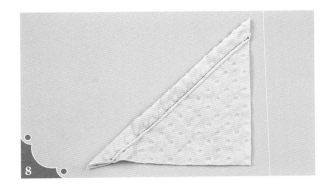

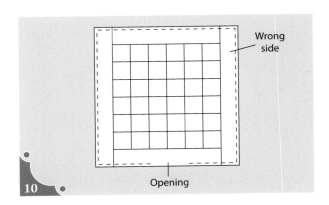

Opening

Wrong side

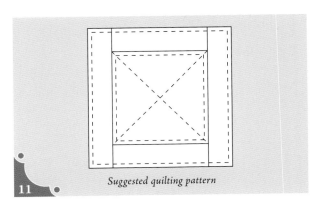

Suggested quilting pattern

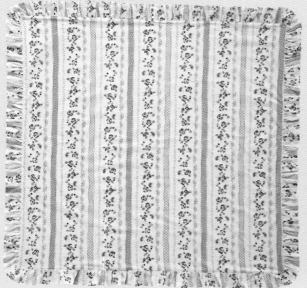

Consider making a patchwork blanket and a receiving blanket as a matching set!

Wrapping Ideas

Now that you have your precious baby gift, let's consider how to wrap it.

Objects as large as quilts usually do not require different packaging since they themselves are beautiful wrappings. One way to wrap a gift like a quilt is to carefully fold it, tie it with a fabric ribbon, and sew a flower to the top as a finishing touch.

The Eva Pouch (page 120) will beautifully encase your gift and can be made very quickly.

Allow me to add one last suggestion. I prefer using tags instead of greeting cards. Tags can later be used as bookmarks, bringing special memories to the recipient.

Photo by Jung W Yang

About the Author

Sue Kim has been designing sought-after creative sewing patterns for many years. She lives in Manitoba, Canada, with her three lovely children and husband. Sue shares her patterns and creativity on her popular website, ithinksew.com. She started sewing when she was ten years old and has always had a passion for crafts. She earned a master's degree in ancient Asian theater. However, she kept sewing and designing as a hobby until, luckily, she was asked to be a sewing instructor at a Jo-Ann Fabric and Craft store. That expanded into requests to teach in several quilt shops. The quilt shop owners also encouraged her to start her own pattern business.

Her first patterns were for small bags and clutches, and eventually she was asked to make a pattern book of bags and clutches. She is the author of *Bags: The Modern Classics* (C&T Publishing). Many of the patterns Sue sells are downloadable PDF patterns. She has completed several books of patterns and has become an independent pattern designer, writing for several publishers and pattern companies.

Sue has countless ideas; her sketchbook is never empty.

Resources

Michael Miller Fabrics, LLC
michaelmillerfabrics.com

Andover
AndoverFabrics.com

Riley Blake
rileyblakedesigns.com

Fat Quarter Shop
fatquartershop.com

Fabricworm / Birch Fabrics
fabricworm.com

Fabric Shoppe
etsy.com/shop/fabricshoppe

Cloud 9 Fabric
cloud9fabrics.com

Previous books by Sue Kim:

stashBOOKS

fabric arts for a handmade lifestyle

If you're craving beautiful authenticity in a time of mass-production...Stash Books is for you. Stash Books is a line of how-to books celebrating fabric arts for a handmade lifestyle. Backed by C&T Publishing's solid reputation for quality, Stash Books will inspire you with contemporary designs, clear and simple instructions, and engaging photography.

www.stashbooks.com